ROBERT E. LEE
IN TEXAS

BY

CARL COKE RISTER

☆

FOREWORD BY

JERRY THOMPSON

UNIVERSITY OF OKLAHOMA PRESS
NORMAN

TO MY FRIEND

Eugene Holman

WHO WAS REARED IN THAT PART OF TEXAS

OVER WHICH LEE PROJECTED HIS

COMANCHE CAMPAIGN OF 1856

Library of Congress Cataloging-in-Publication Data

Rister, Carl Coke, 1889–1955.
    Robert E. Lee in Texas / by Carl Coke Rister
      p.   cm.
    Includes bibliographical references (p.) and index.
    ISBN 0-8061-3642-1 (pbk. : alk. paper)
        1. Lee, Robert E. (Robert Edward), 1807–1870. 2. Texas—
History—1846–1950. 3. Frontier and pioneer life—Texas.
4. Texas—History, Military—19th century. 5. Indians of North
America—Wars—Texas. 6. Indians of North America—Wars—
1815–1875. 7. Texas—Boundaries—Mexico. 8. Mexico—
Boundaries—Texas. 9. Generals—United States—Biography.
I. Title.

E467.1.L4R58 2004
973.6'6'092—dc22
[B]
                                                    2004051737

3   4   5   6   7   8   9   10   11   12

1

Contents

	Foreword to the Paperback Edition	v
I.	*"America's Very Best Soldier"*	3
II.	*Lee's "Texas Home"*	19
III.	*Reconnaissance*	37
IV.	*Along the Rio Grande*	53
V.	*From Pillar to Post*	69
VI.	*"A Desert of Dullness"*	83
VII.	*"That Myth Cortinas"*	96
VIII.	*"A Rough Diplomatist"*	115
IX.	*Camels and Comanches*	126
X.	*Farewell to Texas*	150
	Bibliography	169
	Index	177

Illustrations

Lieutenant Robert E. Lee	*page* 10
Lieutenant Colonel Robert E. Lee	34
Map of Lee's journeys in Texas	41
Military Plaza, San Antonio	50
Drawing of Camp Cooper	57
General George H. Thomas	66
Brownsville, Texas	98
Officers' Quarters, San Antonio	130
Nimitz Hotel, Fredericksburg, Texas	146
Drawing of Fort Mason	152
Arlington	162

Foreword to the
Paperback Edition

THIRTY-EIGHT years after the end of the Civil War, the legislature of the Commonwealth of Virginia agreed to commission two statues to be sent to Washington, D.C., for placement in the capitol. George Washington was an obvious choice, but who would be chosen for the second statue? Passing over such intellectual giants as Thomas Jefferson and James Madison, it was decided the second statue should be of Gen. Robert Edward Lee. Four decades later, President Franklin D. Roosevelt was invited to Dallas, Texas, to unveil a massive statue of the Virginian. By this time, it was evident that Lee had become not only a Virginian and southern idol, but a national hero. Even into the twenty-first century, few names in American history excite the historical imagination as does that of Robert E. Lee. His hold on the American consciousness remains pervasive and grows with the passage of time. To many Americans, Lee remains larger than life.

Countless biographies have portrayed Lee at West Point as the perfect student and have shown how in Mexico he matured into a dedicated soldier, whom Gen. Winfield Scott pronounced the "very best soldier I ever saw in the field." During the Civil War, Lee went on to become the Confederacy's tactical genius and master strategist. Accolades aside, it should be remembered that Lee, despite his flawless character, helped lead a rebellion that his Army of Northern Virginia came close to winning. A resounding Union defeat would probably have led to a southern republic with slavery intact. Moreover, the course of American history would have been radically altered. Yet in the American mind, Lee remains the dashing Virginia cavalier and a national hero.

Of particular interest to scholars and students of Texas and the Southwest has been Carl Coke Rister's *Robert E. Lee in Texas.* Rister came to study and write about Lee after a long and distinguished career of teaching and scholarship. Born in the West Texas hamlet of Hayrick, Rister came of age in sparsely settled Coke County, where his father was a Baptist minister. After high school, he gave serious consideration to becoming a professional baseball player and was even offered a contract by a professional baseball club in Abilene. Instead, Rister went on to receive a bachelor's degree in social science from Simmons College, or what became Hardin-Simmons University, also in Abilene. After writing a thesis on the Ku Klux Klan of Reconstruction, he received his master's degree in history from George Washington University and returned to his original alma mater as an assistant professor of history. Studying for two summers with Herbert Eugene Bolton at the University of California at Berkeley, he became impressed with the opportunities for research and writing in the field of western history. Returning to George Washington University, he completed a dissertation entitled "Texas Frontier Defense, 1865–1881," and received his doctorate in 1925. Back in Abilene, he taught American and European history at Hardin-Simmons, where he was promoted to full professor and where he joined his distinguished colleague, Rupert N. Richardson, in editing the first *Year Book* of the West Texas Historical Association.

While still at Hardin-Simmons, Rister's revised dissertation was published as *The Southwestern Frontier, 1865–1881.* The next year, he was lured to the University of Oklahoma, where he remained for twenty-two years, first as professor of history, then as chairman of the history department, and finally as distinguished Research Professor. As he continued to write and publish, Rister gained a national reputation as a leading authority on the history of the southwestern frontier. Lured back across the Red River to Texas Tech University in 1951, he was named distinguished professor of history. Friendly, neatly dressed, cordial, and a dedicated teacher and researcher, Rister died unexpectedly of a heart attack on April 16, 1955, while spending the night with relatives at Rotan, Texas. His library and papers came to form a large part of the Southwest Collection at Texas Tech, which he had helped promote while at Lubbock.

During his tenures at Norman and Lubbock, Rister published a number of impressive books. With his good friend Rupert Richardson, he coauthored *The Greater Southwest* in 1934. Four years later, his *Southern Plainsmen* was widely read and critically acclaimed. His *Border Captives,* which followed, was a groundbreaking study of an ugly phase in Indian-white relations—the trafficking in prisoners by Native Americans. *Land Hunger* (1942) was the story of David L. Payne and the "Boomers" in the opening of Oklahoma's unassigned lands. *Border Command: General Phil Sheridan in the West* (1944) ably chronicled Sheridan's defeat of the southern Plains Indians. For many years, Rister had studied and wanted to write a book about the oil industry. *Oil! Titan of the Southwest,* which was made possible by a $30,000 grant from the Standard Oil Company of New Jersey, was published in 1949. Although Rister claimed he had never received a bad review, a few critics described this work as oil company propaganda, a charge that deeply hurt Rister. Convinced such charges were unjustified and unfair, he was gratified when other reviewers called it his most distinguished work. Later publications included *Comanche Bondage* (1955) and *Fort Griffin on the Texas Frontier* (1956), both of which were released posthumously. Today, many of Rister's books remain in print.

Certainly one of Rister's most popular and widely read books was his study of Lee, which was published by the University of Oklahoma Press shortly after World War II. Although Rister had already established a reputation as a first-rate narrative historian, *Robert E. Lee in Texas* (1946) was undeniably one of his best. Meticulously researched and exceptionally well written, the book detailed the twenty-five months Lee spent in Texas during the crucial years before the Civil War. Convinced

Lee's reputation did not need defending, Rister provided little analysis or interpretation and did not choose to provide end-notes or footnotes. He was convinced the facts, when presented in a straight-forward manner, would speak for themselves.

For knowledgeable readers, it is readily evident that Rister thoroughly probed various archival collections at the National Archives, Library of Congress, libraries at both the University of Texas and the University of Oklahoma, as well as the Texas State Library, for any relevant documents relating to Lee's stay in Texas. It is also evident that Rister drew heavily on the work and advice of Douglas Southall Freeman, editor of the Richmond *News Leader*, who a decade earlier had written an exhaustively well-researched and award-winning four-volume study of Lee, simply entitled *R. E. Lee*.

Some readers today might question Rister's use of the word "Negro" or his references to Comanches as "greasy and filthy." One must remember that at the time Rister completed his work on Lee, "Negro" was widely accepted and used by black and white scholars and journalists alike. Although Rister's post-World War II academic world was far removed from Lee's slave-holding Virginia, it was, nevertheless, still influenced by segregation and deep-rooted racism.

What is not in question is Rister's superb scholarship. Long before microfilm became readily available by interlibrary loan, Rister spent weeks in Washington, D.C., and elsewhere, carefully examining Lee's personal papers, or any historical collection that might shed light on Lee's tour of duty in Texas. Going beyond Freeman's *R. E. Lee* in detailing Lee's career in the Lone Star State, Rister's *Robert E. Lee in Texas* is a study of remarkable depth.

As a devout Baptist who professed faith in hard work and virtue, Rister greatly admired Lee, seeing the Virginian as part of an evolutionary process on the Texas frontier that pitted good against evil. To Rister, Lee was a model of honesty, simplicity, and an individual devoid of personal problems, devoted to God and country. He was a high-stepping Virginia cavalier sent to tame a rough and violent Texas frontier. In *Robert E. Lee in Texas,*

Rister gives us the traditional Lee of the "Lost Cause," a soldier without fault or imperfection. Lee on the Texas frontier, in Rister's eyes, was the embodiment of Manifest Destiny, a knight-crusader striving to change a howling wilderness into a place fit for civilized man.

In reality, as the scholar Thomas L. Connelly has so ably demonstrated in his *Marble Man: Robert E. Lee and His Image in American Society,* Lee was a far more complex individual, someone who was full of self-doubt, frustration, and fearful of failure, traits that may have been inherited from his father, Gen. Henry "Light-Horse Harry" Lee, a vain and ambitious man, who suffered through two sentences in a debtor prison. Having a strong Calvinistic obsession with sin and caught in an unsatisfactory marriage, Lee, especially on the Texas frontier, suffered from boredom and loneliness. But in all fairness, most soldiers on the vast Texas frontier of the 1850s were also prone to bouts of melancholy and frequently longed to return to their families in the East.

During the four years before Confederates at Charleston, South Carolina, inaugurated the Civil War, Lee spent over two years of his life in Texas. These months were full of enough high drama to captivate anyone interested in Lee or the history of the Lone Star State. Rister first takes us to Camp Cooper on the Clear Fork of the Brazos River where Lee ably commanded two squadrons of the elite Second United States Cavalry. Here on the bleak and dusty West Texas prairie, he struggled to adapt himself to routine post life at his "Texas home," amusing himself as best he could, even keeping a rattlesnake as a pet. There was also court-martial duty on the distant Rio Grande at Fort Ringgold, Fort Brown, and at Indianola on the wind-swept Texas coast.

From the Texas frontier, in search of hostile Comanches, Lee in 1866 led four squadrons of the Second Cavalry on a forty-day, 1,600-mile expedition to the headwaters of the Colorado and Brazos rivers and the vast Llano Estacado. Later, while in San Antonio, Lee was called back to Virginia to administer the estate of his deceased father-in-law. While at Arlington House in October 1859, he was thrust into history once again when orders arrived sending him to Harpers Ferry, Virginia, where a radical abolitionist named John Brown had attacked the federal arsenal. Back in San Antonio and in command of the Department of Texas, Lee was ordered south to the Mexican border through a frigid Texas norther. In Brownsville, a wily and crafty *tejano,* Juan Nepomuceno Cortina, had shot up the town and instigated a bloody war on the Rio Grande.

At regimental headquarters at Fort Mason, two miles west of Comanche Creek and eight miles above its confluence with the Llano River in Mason County, with war clouds lowering over a troubled and beleaguered nation, Lee was ordered back to Washington. Arriving in San Antonio in February 1861, before traveling east, Lee pulled his ambulance up in front of the Read House only to notice the streets swarming with zealous young Texans wearing red insignia on their coats or shirts. Told they were state troops and that Gen. David E. Twiggs had surrendered the Department of Texas, Lee's eyes clouded with tears. "Has it come to this," he was heard to whisper. Back on the banks of the Potomac at Arlington House, the Virginian confided to a friend that had he been in command in Texas at the time of the Twiggs surrender, he would not have capitulated. If Lee had indeed been in command in San Antonio, the ruinous and catastrophic war that followed would likely have commenced in Texas, rather than at Fort Sumter eight weeks later. Moreover, Lee at the head of an army in blue could have been a distinct possibility.

In Washington, Lee was called to the office of Gen. Winfield Scott on Pennsylvania Avenue where he was offered command of the Union Army. As every clear-eyed southern schoolboy knows, Lee declined, refusing to lift "his sword against his native Virginia." The rest is history. But before the long road to Appomattox Court House, be prepared to ride with Lee as he masters the vast and uncivilized Texas frontier.

JERRY THOMPSON

Texas A&M International University

Preface

FOR twenty-five months of the four turbulent years just before the Civil War, Lieutenant Colonel Robert Edward Lee saw service in Texas—at Camp Cooper, watching the federal government's "humanizing" experiment with the wild Comanches; at San Antonio, commanding the Department of Texas; and at Fort Mason, headquarters of the Second Cavalry. Not only for the nation but for Lee were these critical years. To move from West Point, steeped in American military tradition, a setting of culture and refinement, to Camp Cooper on an Indian frontier, where isolation, rawness, inconvenience, deprivation, and even death were commonplaces, was indeed revolutionary. Lee had never before known primitive life, and to be catapulted into it now staggered his whole being. That he made the necessary adjustment and that on a lonely frontier he found peace, strength, and wisdom proved his qualities of greatness.

Three positive results came from Lee's Texas services. First, he worked with, and for the most part commanded, the famous Second United States Cavalry, most of the officers of which a few years later became either Northern or Southern field commanders. To know these officers, their points of strength and points of weakness, their whims and caprices, and their likes and dislikes served him well in military crises. Second, he found the frontier so primitive that he must adjust himself to elemental circumstances, must adapt himself to outdoor life and adverse conditions such as he would meet on Civil War battle fields. And third, absence made his heart grow fonder of his family, his home, and Virginia. Lee loved the Union dearly, but when he was faced with the choice of remaining in it and serving as its military leader or of going with Virginia in secession, he felt compelled to defend Virginia, his family, and his home.

While camping in the silent wastes of Texas, while at San Antonio or at a border post, he had opportunity to consider his dilemma; and there is little doubt that these Texas experiences helped him to make his decision. They gave point to his wisdom and brought self-mastery, qualities which his junior officers admired and of which they stood in awe. When he came from the Texas wilderness to report to General Scott in Washington, he was prepared to assume the role of the South's peerless leader.

The author feels grateful for services rendered him by others in the assembling of materials for this study. A grant-in-aid was given by the University of Oklahoma Faculty Research Committee for study in Washington, D. C. The staffs of the National Archives, the Library of Congress, the Texas State Library, the University of Texas Library, and the University of Oklahoma Library were courteous and helpful in making available bodies of manuscript and documentary and out-of-print materials. Mrs. Hanson Ely and Mrs. Hunter DeButts graciously consented that the author examine the restricted Lee family papers in the Division of Manuscripts, Library of Congress. Others who furnished materials or who gave expert advice were Harriet Smither, Austin, Texas; Henry Sayles, Jr., Abilene, Texas; Richard H. Shoemaker, Acting Librarian, Cyrus Hall McCormick Library, Washington and Lee University, Lexington, Virginia; C. L. Greenwood, Austin, Texas; Colonel M. L. Crimmins, San Antonio, Texas; and Dr. George Bolling Lee, New York City. The author feels particularly indebted to Douglas Southall Freeman, editor of the Richmond *News Leader,* not only for the wealth of detail and bibliography found in his definitive biography of Lee but also for his encouraging advice.

CARL COKE RISTER

Norman, Oklahoma
February 5, 1946

Robert E. Lee in Texas

"America's Very Best Soldier"

THROUGHOUT the day of April 9, 1856, Lieutenant Colonel Robert Edward Lee's small train of seven wagons, escorted by a corporal and eight soldiers, had crawled northward, bouncing and jouncing over an uneven Texas frontier road, uphill and downhill, across creeks and ravines, and occasionally through post-oak flats carpeted with green grass and yellow splashes of the spring's first primroses. Toward the close of day, the tired men crossed a mesquite tableland and approached a steep bluff overlooking the Clear Fork of the Brazos River, thirty-five miles above its junction with the Brazos. From this vantage point Lee saw before him a wide, level valley, through which flowed the meandering river. Gnarled mesquite trees, dwarfed and drought-blighted, chaparral, stunted hackberry, and prickly pear covered its grassy bottom, except along the river where tall and wide-spreading elm and pecan trees with tender green buds and new leaves furnished a pleasing backdrop. Chrome- and gray-streaked cliffs stood back on either side of the valley like medieval battlemented walls.

Brakes shrieked their protest as the heavily laden wagons slid down the steeply inclined road to the crossing of the clear-running stream. But the drivers urged their teams through the water and up the opposite bank. There ahead, in the upper part of the valley, gleamed white army tents, neatly arranged about a small parade ground.

This was Camp Cooper—named in honor of Adjutant General Samuel Cooper—a military camp, two miles above the agency of the Comanche reservation recently made possible by a Texas legislative grant and surveyed by Captain Randolph B. Marcy and Special Agent Robert S. Neighbors, representing the United States government. Here, at this secluded and remote place, the federal government proposed to teach these nomadic red men the ways of their white neighbors, under the strict watch of the near-by soldiers.

At last Lee had completed his journey from Fort Mason, 165 miles to the south. He had made a radical change in military command—from the superintendency of West Point, where he had most recently served with distinction and where, years before, he had received his military education, to the wild Texas frontier. This was the West, stripped of the glamour that it might have had for him when he made his first acquaintance with Texas during the war with Mexico.

Lee's background was not such as to fit him ideally for border life. A Virginian, son of General Henry ("Light Horse Harry") Lee and Ann Carter Lee, he had received his early training at Alexandria and had finished second in a class of forty-six at West Point. Then as an officer of the Corps of Engineers he had served with conspicuous success at Cockspur Island, in the Savannah River, Georgia; at Fort Monroe, Virginia; at Washington as assistant

4

to the Chief of Engineers, Charles Gratiot; at St. Louis, where he had changed the channel of the Mississippi River; and at Fort Hamilton, New York, where he had been stationed when the Mexican War called him to Texas. His devotion to duty by this time had brought promotion from second lieutenant to captain.

Beyond these military experiences, one other event stands out during these early years as life-shaping for young Lee. On June 30, 1831, he married Mary Custis, daughter of George Washington Parke Custis, the adopted son of George Washington. Mary's home, stately old Arlington, on Virginia Heights overlooking the broad, placid Potomac and Washington beyond, was aglow the night of the wedding. It had never before been the scene of a happier gathering, its widespread wings serving as open arms to welcome the guests. The massive but simple Doric columns of the broad portico graced the occasion with a classic air. The great halls and chambers, decorated with paintings of patriots and scenes of the Revolution, rang with laughter and music; and history and tradition breathed their legends upon a canvas softer than a dream of peace.

Douglas Southall Freeman says significantly that Lee married Arlington when he married Mary Custis. Indeed, both the young bride and her home helped direct his mental and spiritual growth in later years. Arlington bound his cultural love to the proud Washington heritage; and he shared with Mary the care and rearing of a large family: three sons (George Washington Custis, William Fitzhugh, and Robert Edward) and four daughters (Mary, Annie, Agnes, and Mildred). That he provided cultural and material advantages for them from a slender income proved that his genius did not lie wholly in the military field.

Dull routine plagued ambitious Lee while he was stationed at Fort Hamilton. He fretted, fumed, and fidgeted, hoping for a change and advancement. But occasionally he was in a happier mood. On January 14, 1846, he wrote Mary that he had kept his servants, Jim and "Miss Leary," constantly moving, cleaning up, and he feared that he would wear them down. "I do not know whether it was your departure or my somber phiz," he added, "which brought Miss Leary out Sunday in a full suit of mourning. A black alpaca trimmed with crepe and a thick row of jet buttons on each sleeve, from the shoulder to the wrist, and three rows on the skirt, diverging from the waist to the hem; it was, however, surmounted by a dashing cap with gay ribbons."

From Fort Hamilton Lee watched with interest the rising tide of "manifest destiny," the crest of which was soon to bear him to Texas. He saw the Democrats send the Tennessean, James K. Polk, to the White House in Washington on the militant slogans, "Fifty-four forty or fight" and "Reannexation of Texas." Then he was stirred by the action of Congress annexing Texas by a joint resolution and by Mexico's severance of diplomatic relations with the United States. Hastily England now agreed to accept the forty-ninth parallel as her Oregon boundary rather than risk a fight for "Fifty-four forty." This, too, must have impressed Lee.

War, following a bitter quarrel between Mexico and the United States, brought Lee to Texas the first time. General Zachary Taylor's army had clashed with Arista's forces on May 8 and 9, 1846, at Palo Alto and Resaca de la Palma, after which the Americans had crossed the Rio Grande and had occupied Matamoros and Monterrey. At the same time Brigadier General John E. Wool, whom Lee had formerly known in Virginia, was busy at San Antonio organizing a second army to aid Taylor. Lee's fretting and fuming now ended, for he was sent to Texas to assist Wool. On the first available steamer he sailed via New Orleans for Port Lavaca, Texas, and from there rode on to San Antonio on September 21.

This was Lee's first visit to San Antonio, a town of a few more than 2,000 inhabitants, yet drowsy in spite of its part in creating the lusty young republic. The battle-scarred Alamo, where a decade earlier James Bowie and his brave Texans had been slaughtered by Santa Anna's storming troops; the century-old San Fernando Church, with four older missions within easy walking distance; the flat-topped adobe shops and business houses and the Governor's Palace; narrow and crooked streets, littered with refuse; and indolent Mexicans, lounging in door-ways of jacales and adobe huts and attired in bell-bottom trousers, tight-fitting jackets, serapes, and sombreros— all Lee saw as an interesting past. Yet he found, too, that this drowsy air had been rudely jolted by the bustle and confusion of war. Smartly-dressed officers rode excitedly here and there, anxious to complete arrangements for the army's march southward; and Wool's train of 500 wagons moved to and fro between San Antonio and La-vaca, bringing up supplies.

Wool assigned Lee to an important role. He was to assist Captain William D. Fraser in collecting tools for road- and bridge-building and pontoons to throw across the Rio Grande. Then these engineers were to push on to improve the road over which the army would march to Eagle Pass. This assignment was no mean task, for Wool had assembled for the start an army of 2,829 men, more than 2,000 horses, and 1,112 wagons; and the road to be made ready was between 175 and 185 miles in length. Lee and Fraser, with a work crew, left the Alamo city on September 23 and performed their task so well that on November 9 Wool's army reached the Rio Grande, about thirty miles south of what is now Eagle Pass. Here the two engineers put up their pontoons and made their bridge ready for the crossing. The Mexican troops guarding the passage retired without firing a shot.

From the river crossing Wool pushed on through mesquite and cactus flats and over rugged terrain, his men suffering from the intense heat and dust. To add to the misery, for a part of the way each man's ration was limited to nine ears of corn per day. The army passed through Monclova, a town of 10,000 inhabitants, and through Parras, of 5,000, still without meeting an enemy. Lee had worked hard, had solved every construction problem given him, and was tired; but he was given little time to rest. General Worth at Saltillo sent Wool an urgent appeal for help because Santa Anna was reported to be advancing with a large army. Again Lee and Fraser moved out to make ready the uncertain road between Parras and Saltillo, and again they did their work well.

When the travel-worn soldiers reached Agua Nueva, near Saltillo, and made contact with Worth's army, they found everyone extremely nervous, from Worth down to his buck privates. On one day a cloud of dust raised by an American cavalry patrol had been mistaken for the

Mexicans; and on another, Santa Anna had been reported to be near.

Lee went to reconnoiter, when Wool refused to believe this last report. He was to meet his escort beyond the picket line, but when he came to the selected spot at the designated time, his men had not appeared. Impatient, he rode on without them, accompanied only by a Mexican guide whom he had impressed into service by the show of two heavy cavalry pistols. Twenty miles from camp, in late evening, he saw ahead the twinkling lights of what he thought might be Santa Anna's campfires. His guide thought so, too, and refused to go farther. Stealthily Lee moved on alone and soon found that this was a camp of harmless sheepherders, who told him that Santa Anna was yet far to the south. With this news Lee rode back late that night to Wool's camp to report to his alarmed chief. He was amused to find that Wool had arrested the guide's father and had threatened to hang him if Lee did not return unharmed.

Here Lee's services with Wool's army ended. He could feel justly proud of his part in making possible the army's remarkable journey, which Colonel M. L. Crimmins states "for sheer audacity and rigid discipline . . . ranks with the heroic march of Xenophon." The Americans had traversed a semidesert for almost 700 miles, over hastily-improved roads made ready by Lee and Fraser. Swift rivers had been bridged, hills leveled, and mountains made passable. No wreckage marked the route, not a drop of blood was shed, and not a shot was fired!

On January 16, 1847, Lee rode Creole, his favorite mare, northward to join General Winfield ("Fuss and Feathers") Scott's army concentrating at Brazos Santiago,

Texas, opposite the mouth of the Rio Grande. From Brazos Santiago, Scott sailed for Vera Cruz, stopping en route only long enough to occupy Tampico. Lee and his friend, Joseph E. Johnston, sailed with the convoy aboard the *Massachusetts,* their horses following on another ship.

Lee now began a series of brilliant achievements—at Vera Cruz, at Cerro Gordo, at Jalapa, Contreras, San Antonio, and Churubusco—that brought him special mention, again and again, from General Scott. His skill and reckless daring were so conspicuous, according to E. D. Keyes, as to cause Scott to have an "almost idolatrous fancy for Lee, whose military genius he estimated far above that of any other officer of the army." Lee was brevetted a major for gallant and meritorious conduct at Cerro Gordo, a lieutenant colonel for conspicuous heroism at Contreras and Churubusco, and a colonel for his bravery and skill at Chapultepec. And as though this were not enough, Scott shortly proclaimed him "America's very best soldier."

Lee took these promotions and plaudits soberly. The horrible realism of war had shocked him immeasurably. At Vera Cruz he had described the fire power of 32- and 68-pound cannon as "awful!" "It was terrible to think of the women and children," he wrote Mrs. Lee. Each added experience was much the same—horror, chaos, the stench of death, bloated and disfigured bodies, shrieks of the wounded, moans of the dying, and the weeping of women and children beside the still forms of the dead. As with a branding iron, Lee's soul was seared. At battle-littered Cerro Gordo he had rescued from under the dead body of a large Mexican soldier a young bugler, who lay suffering with a shattered arm while his little sister stood

LIEUTENANT ROBERT E. LEE
at the time of his marriage in 1831

by weeping. "Her large black eyes were streaming with tears," Lee wrote, "her hands crossed over her breast." After he had sent the lad to a first-aid station and had ridden away, the girl's plaintive *"Mille gracias, Señor"* rang in his ears hauntingly. Creole, too, seemed to understand and stepped gingerly over the dead men as if she feared to hurt them. "You have no idea what a horrible sight a battlefield is," Lee wrote Mary, "with musket balls and grapes in perfect showers whistling overhead on their errands of death."

But on these battle fields Lee "marched, bivouacked, fought and bled" (for he was wounded) side by side with such men as Joseph E. Johnston, George B. McClellan, P. G. T. Beauregard, and Joseph Hooker, men whom he was to know on Civil War battle fields either as Northern or Southern commanders. No one knows how important this knowledge was to Lee. Certainly, he only heard of, and did not know personally, some of those men he would serve with or meet as foes. It is safe to assume, however, that his plans for the Peninsula campaign and for Chancellorsville, during 1862–63, were at least in part shaped because of his having known McClellan and Hooker.

While Lee awaited the conclusion of peace negotiations following the Mexican War, he could hear in camp the strains of "Home, Sweet Home." "We feel quite exhilirated at the prospect of getting home," he wrote his brother, Smith. Too much debate in the Mexican Congress irritated him; it was too late to argue about who had begun the war. He believed that American troops had won fairly and had the right to exact concessions. "The treaty gives us all the land we want," he explained further. "The amount we pay is a trifle, and is the cheapest way of ending the war. How it will all end I cannot say, but will trust to a kind Providence, who will, I believe, order all things for the best." He little realized that the total direct and indirect war costs would reach 12,000 lives and $100,000,000, and that the region acquired was two and one-half times as large as France.

As Lee watched for a homeward-bound steamer, the American press, led by the Washington *Union,* pictured the American and Mexican eagles clasping wings and praised the Yankee doughboys for swapping knickknacks with the Mexican *rancheros.*

Early in June, 1848, Lee boarded the long-awaited steamer at Vera Cruz, and late in the month he completed his journey by riding horseback from Washington to Arlington. His faithful dog, Spec, was the first to see him and to bark a welcome, much to the surprise of his waiting family, who, having sent a carriage to Washington for him, had not expected him to return in this fashion. The Lee children hardly knew the sober, bronzed man who stood before them: war had penciled deep lines of care on his face, and sadness had crept into his eyes. He caught up a small boy and kissed him, only to discover that he was not his own; he had mistaken little Armistead Lippitt for his son, Rob, who was standing by anxiously, clothed in his best for the occasion. But the error was immediately corrected, and soon Lee was happily embracing all and distributing presents he had brought from Mexico. "Here I am once again," he wrote his brother, Smith, "perfectly surrounded by Mary and her precious children, who seem to devote themselves to staring at the furrows in my face and the white hairs in my head."

Scott rewarded Lee for his brilliant Mexican War services by an appointment to the superintendency of West Point, where he spent a little more than two busy years (September 1, 1852 to April 12, 1855) in improving the school's discipline and its course of study and in planning for expansion. These were happy and profitable months that ended all too soon. Not only had they reunited Lee and his family, but he had formed new friendships among his faculty and students that were to last through the years. He knew as students such men as John B. McPherson, William R. Boggs, John B. Hood, "Jeb" Stuart, Archibald Gracie, W. D. Pender, O. O. Howard, and Phil Sheridan. George H. Thomas, an instructor in artillery and cavalry, he would soon meet again on the Texas frontier; and the others, his students, as friends or foes on the Civil War battle fields.

Border events brought a radical change in Lee's military life and turned his eyes again toward Texas. In the midsummer of 1854, Indians had ambushed Lieutenant John L. Grattan's patrol near Fort Laramie, Wyoming. Only one man had escaped alive, and even he had died of his wounds a short time later. This massacre added weight to Secretary Davis's recent request of Congress for two new cavalry regiments. The Secretary had pointed out that the widely distributed army of 11,000 officers and men hardly protected a frontier of 8,000 miles against 40,000 hostile warriors. The Grattan massacre furnished tragic proof of this, and on March 3, 1855, Congress went beyond Davis's request by authorizing two new regiments of cavalry and two of infantry.

One of these, the Second Cavalry, was to patrol the Texas border. Fortunately Secretary Davis, a West Pointer, selected its officers; and never before in American annals had such talented men been chosen. Albert Sidney Johnston was named colonel; Lee, lieutenant colonel; William J. Hardee and George H. Thomas, majors; and among its captains were Earl Van Dorn, E. Kirby Smith, N. G. Evans, I. N. Palmer, George Stoneman, and R. W. Johnson. Even its lieutenants—John B. Hood, Charles W. Field, William P. Chambliss, Charles W. Phifer, and K. Garrard—rose to high rank during the Civil War, either as Confederate or Union officers. Hardee, Van Dorn, Smith, Evans, Field, Hood, Chambliss and Phifer became well-known Southern generals; and Thomas, Palmer, Stoneman, R. W. Johnson, and Garrard, Northern generals.

Lee frowned on a transfer from staff to line. Border duty meant separation from his family and home, a radical change from a quiet, comfortable station in an eastern city to a crude border post. Still he could not expect promotion with the Corps of Engineers—too many officers outranked him. With the new regiment he had a chance even for a brigadier generalship. In addition, his sense of duty compelled him to accept the appointment. Therefore, on March 23 he turned over his West Point command to Brevet Major Jonathan G. Barnard and left for his home to spend a few days with his family before starting west.

Three weeks later Lee received orders to take command of the Second Cavalry being assembled at Louisville, Kentucky, since Johnston was not ready for duty. A short time afterward he moved the regiment to Jefferson Barracks, Missouri, to drill his troopers. His work was discouraging. "Ague, cholera and desertion" demoralized his men. "Yesterday at muster," he wrote Mrs. Lee, "I found one of the late arrivals in a dirty, tattered shirt and pants, with a white hat and shoes, with other garments to match. I asked him why he did not put on clean clothes. He said he had none. I asked him if he could not wash and mend those. He said he had nothing else to put on. I then told him immediately after muster to go down to the river, wash his clothes, and sit on the bank and watch the passing steamboats till they dried, and then mend them. This morning at inspection he looked as proud as possible, stood in the position of a soldier with his little fingers on the seams of his pants, his beaver cocked back, and his toes sticking through his shoes, but his skin and solitary two garments clean. He grinned very happily at my compliments."

Dull, dreary court-martial duty broke in on the Jefferson Barracks routine to prevent Lee's journey southward with his regiment. Such irksome service sometimes made necessary hundreds of miles of riding, living in the open or in a tent, and tedious hours of listening to witnesses and the arguments of advocates. Lee had six such assignments, beginning in September, 1855. Johnston wrote that he, too, was "annoyed" by having to serve at Fort Leavenworth, Kansas, on the September hearing against several officers. Next, Lee moved on to Fort Riley, farther west in the same state, to sit in judgment on an army surgeon who had deserted his post of duty during an epidemic. Then in January, 1856, he journeyed eastward to Carlisle Barracks, Pennsylvania; and from there, to West Point. Fortunately, the last assignment brought Lee near Arlington and permitted him to visit with his family again before he started for Texas.

15

Meanwhile, in October, 1855, Johnston had marched to Texas at the head of the Second Cavalry. From Jefferson Barracks he and his men rode through the Ozarks of southwestern Missouri, by way of Springfield and Neosho, into Indian Territory. Through this territory they traveled via Tahlequah, Fort Gibson, and Fort Washita to Preston on the Red River; from there they moved over the military road to Fort Mason, Texas, passing through Fort Belknap and Camp Cooper.

After they had left Preston for Belknap, they were overtaken by a norther that sent the mercury tumbling and the men shivering. Johnston wrote: "Norther! It makes me cold to write the word. I do not believe that any of the hyperborean explorers felt the cold more intensely than did my regiment. Noble fellows! Officers and men, they will always be found at their post, wherever duty calls them. Think of a northern blast, sixty miles an hour, unceasing, unrelenting (the mercury below zero, ice six inches thick), coming suddenly down on the highest tableland of Texas, 2,000 feet above the sea." On December 23 the cavalry sought safety behind a "skirt of timber"; but on the following day, when it resumed its march, it was overtaken by hail, snow, and sleet, and both men and animals suffered intensely. A wagon train on its way from the Texas coast to meet them had lost 113 oxen.

Johnston left Major Hardee and two squadrons of troopers at Camp Cooper to assist the new Comanche agent, John R. Baylor; and he and the other companies moved on southward via Fort Chadbourne to Fort Mason, which they reached on January 14, 1856.

Lee had parted from Mary and the children at Arlington on February 12. When he registered at the Plaza

Hotel in San Antonio twenty-four days later, he had completed a difficult journey from Indianola while the roads were quagmires. When his wagon would hit a bog, he would leap to the ground and trudge through the mud, regardless of the depth, with breeches rolled up to his boot tops.

But as on the occasion of his first visit, Lee did not tarry long. He renewed acquaintance with Colonels Myers and Porter and with officers of lesser rank and was entertained at the Masons' home. Mrs. Mason's two daughters, Lee wrote Mary, were skillful and useful. They made their own dresses and baked "the most beautiful bread, rolls, biscuit and cake."

Although the weather was unfavorable, a few days later Lee began his journey toward Fort Mason with his wagon train. Each afternoon at two o'clock he pitched camp to allow his animals to graze beside the road before nightfall; as a result he did not reach Fort Mason until March 25. There he visited in Colonel and Mrs. Johnston's home. "Mrs. Johnston is a pretty and sweet woman," Lee informed his wife, "intelligent and well adapted to her position and life. She teaches her own children—two boys and a girl—and occupies herself in painting birds and flowers of the country."

A few days later Lee resumed his journey to Camp Cooper, to which Johnston had assigned him. Before leaving, he nailed to the end-gate of one of his wagons a coop of seven hens, which furnished him eggs for the trip.

He found Camp Cooper a lonely border post, eighteen hundred miles from Arlington, Mary, and the children! When would he see them again? Did this constitute a detour in his military career? Lee must have turned these thoughts over in his mind during his first night at his new post. And no doubt he gave them more attention than the unusual sounds—the measured tread of the guard, the staccato bark of the coyotes, the hoot of an owl, or the wind sighing through the mesquite flat. He had begun an experience quite unlike any other of his varied career, one that would condition his body, mind, and soul for later years.

★ II ★

Lee's "Texas Home"

THIS was Lee's first field command—four companies of the Second Cavalry! He was on a raw frontier amid homespun men. His situation gave him anxious concern. Army officers on the border, far away from the amenities of civilization, were inclined to be a rough lot; drinking, gambling, and carousing were common, in the absence of other forms of social activities and entertainment. But Lee was known as the "gentleman soldier," the "best-read man in the army," a "puritan," and he was as much at home in the drawing room as on the drill field. Could he, with this background, hold the respect of his brother officers, of his enlisted men? Certainly his splendid Mexican War record and his West Point superintendency were to his advantage.

He spent the morning following his arrival at Camp Cooper in conferring with Hardee and other officers of the post, most of whom he had known at Jefferson Barracks or elsewhere. Then Katumse came, greasy and filthy, undoubtedly embracing Lee, as was his custom. Agent John R. Baylor had probably sent him. Lee received him unceremoniously. Katumse assured him "volubly and tediously" that the Comanches were the white men's friends and had accepted their customs. But Lee, "very sententious," retorted that he would regard him as such only as long as he deserved his friendship, and that he would meet him "as an enemy the first moment he failed to keep his word." This warning was not what Katumse had expected to hear, and he went away perplexed.

The next day Lee returned Katumse's call, and what he saw and heard must have given him, for the first time, a realistic conception of his new task. In the past his engineering problems had been concrete and physical and had required the application of well-known mathematical formulas and rules; but here must be solved human equations, involving intangible cultural factors, for which there were no known rules.

Katumse's village was typically Comanche. Wolflike dogs, lean and snarling, snapped at the visitor's heels; and the air was filled with a bedlam of noises. The village, comprising about one hundred lodges, whose irregular spacing was wholly unlike that of the tents in Lee's army camp, sprawled for a great distance along the river. Only Katumse's teepee, standing conspicuously apart and decorated with red and yellow pictographs, differed from the others. The whole scene bespoke primitiveness and poverty. That these were buffalo Indians was indicated by their skin lodges, meagerly furnished—a skin mat on the dirt floor, robes for bedding piled in one corner, parfleche bags, thongs, ropes, and other belongings. In front of each family lodge or in an adjacent, smaller lodge was a smoke-blackened meat pot suspended from a tripod over a fire, and near by thin strips of buffalo or deer meat hung from a scaffold, drying in the sun. Lee found a total lack of order—bones carelessly strewn, camp refuse, and swarms of flies.

Unkempt children, evidencing malnutrition, quite

unlike the Virginia children Lee knew, peered from lodges or played near the village. Indian men and women, stolid and indifferent, were engaged with domestic tasks or lounged about, watching him curiously. His visit was short and unpromising. Katumse greeted him as before and expected Lee to observe a ceremonial rite of disrobing, but he removed only his necktie.

Katumse had six wives, some of whom were riding in and out of camp. They did not impress the visitor favorably. He wrote Mary that their paint and ornaments "rendered them more hideous than nature made them." Indeed, he found the whole tribe "extremely uninteresting," far more so than he had ever conceived, and returned to his camp with a feeling that the government's experiment was ill advised.

On the morning of April 13 Lee assisted Major Hardee in checking out prior to his departure for Fort Mason on the following Monday. Many other duties awaited him, the most immediate of which was inspection. Before the morning was far gone, therefore, he stepped from his tent to meet the two squadrons of the Second Cavalry (12 commissioned officers and 226 enlisted men) drawn up on the small parade ground. For Lee this was an important occasion, and he was meticulously and correctly groomed. His soldiers would be as interested in the man who was to lead them through fair and foul weather and stress and strife, as he was in studying their qualities.

It is reasonable to suppose that he did not disappoint them, for he was a man of striking military bearing. He was five feet, eleven inches tall and weighed 175 pounds. His brown eyes, set in a broadly rounded face, with prominent brows and wide temples, normally beamed with gentleness and benevolence. He had black hair streaked with gray, and he was clean shaven except for a black mustache which covered his thin upper lip and extended half an inch beyond the corners of his mouth. He had fine teeth, vision, and hearing, and a voice of lower middle register, rich and resonant. His massive torso rose from narrow hips; his hands were large, but his feet were unusually small; and his legs were flat—well suited for a cavalryman. His hair was parted low on the right side and fluffed above the right ear, and from the part it swept to the left across his forehead and turned up, curling above his left ear.

This morning's inspection was more than routine, and Lee went about it carefully and appraisingly. As he looked at the bronzed, border-seasoned men before him, he was pleased. Amidst a primitive wildness, here was military pageantry unsurpassed, and he must have gazed on it pridefully. Other than their shoes, his troopers' attire was as showy as the dragoons', the only difference being trimmings of yellow instead of orange. Even the cavalry horses, no one of which had cost less than $150, fitted into this colorful setting. Those ridden by troopers of Company A were grays; those of E, sorrels; those of F, bays; and those of K, roans—all well curried and in good fettle.

Lee next inspected his men and their equipment. His four company captains were all distinguished soldiers. Three—Earl Van Dorn, George Stoneman, and Charles J. Whiting—were West Pointers. Van Dorn had been cited for valor in four Mexican War battles and had been secretary of the Louisiana Pascagoula Military Academy when he was called to the Second Cavalry. Whiting had served in the Florida Seminole War and as an assistant engineer on the American-Mexican boundary survey of 1849. Stoneman was also a Mexican War veteran, having marched with the Mormon Battalion to California and later having acted as aide-de-camp to Wool. Theodore O'Hara had not attended West Point, but he was a ripe scholar, a modest gentleman, a Mexican War veteran, and author of "The Bivouac of the Dead" and other poems. Assisting each of these were competent junior officers.

The enlisted personnel came from several states and sections of the country, some even from Mexican battle fields. For the most part, those of Company A were recruited in Alabama ("Alabama Grays"); those of Company E, in Missouri; of Company F, in Kentucky; and of Company K, in Ohio. Already they had become acquainted with routine duties—guarding supply and emigrant trains and mail coaches and scouting. Each man was furnished a brass-mounted Campbell saddle with wooden stirrups, or Grimbsby equipment; a spring, movable stock, or Perry carbine; a Colt navy revolver and dragoon saber, carried by saber belt and carbine sling; a gutta-percha cartridge box; and a cape or talma, with loose sleeves extending to the knees. He wore pale blue trousers, a close-fitting dark blue jacket trimmed with yellow braid, a silken sash, a black hat with looped "eagle at the right side" with trailing ostrich plumes on the left. On his shoulders he had brass scales to turn saber strokes of the enemy. He wore no boots or gauntlets.

Lee must have been pleased by his inspection. And after he had completed it, he could then turn with confidence to other daily tasks.

Before joining with other border commanders in patrol work, Lee set to work to study the defense system of Texas. The immense task of the Second Cavalry in helping to defend the frontier appalled him. The state had an area of 237,000 square miles, or about 150,000,000 acres. Across it, from the Red River to the Rio Grande, stretched an irregular border line of settlements, with arms of occupation here and there reaching up fertile river valleys still farther west. Well in front of the border stood isolated army posts, like lonely sentinels. The map showed why it was possible for Comanche and Kiowa marauders to slip past cavalry patrols undetected. At points, the distance from one post to another was two hundred miles; and numerous hills, canyons, waterless badlands, and dense forests afforded the Indians many approaches.

Lee found three systems of Texas forts. The federal government had established the first system to keep its annexation promise to Texas. These posts—Mason, Croghan, Graham, Worth, and Gates—stood now well among the westernmost settlements, so rapid had been the occupation of the state's domain. But west of these, and beyond the frontier, were newer posts—Belknap, Camp Cooper, Phantom Hill, Chadbourne, Camp Colorado, and McKavett. Farther south, to guard the Rio Grande frontier from Brownsville to El Paso, were Forts Brown, Ringgold Barracks, McIntosh, Davis, and others.

It was apparent now why he, the regiment's second-ranking officer, had been sent to Camp Cooper. Cavalry units here not only shared in reconnaissances and patrol work but also saw that the government's "humanizing" experiment with the wild Comanches was given a fair trial. No doubt General Scott had ordered this.

At Camp Cooper, Lee must so lose himself in his work that his sense of loneliness would be smothered. His deep love for his family, his longing for Virginia and army friends, and his great interest in national affairs, all caused him to feel his border isolation most keenly. But at least he could be with this family in spirit and could glean from the Alexandria *Gazette* the trend of state and national events. He would hide occasional heartache and loneliness in letter writing.

Lee's task was understandable to him only in terms of the federal government's attempts to solve the long-standing Comanche raiding problem, including Captain R. B. Marcy's and Supervising Agent R. S. Neighbors's work in locating the Comanche reservation on the Clear Fork.

He could well appreciate why Comanche hostility had risen in proportion to the westward advance of the settlements, for that advance had been at Indian expense. Surveyors had claimed the Comanches' choicest hunting grounds for future homesites, and white hunters had killed their game. Lee learned, too, why the Comanches were gravely alarmed because of the disappearance of wild game: their families were entirely dependent on the buffalo, elk, and deer.

For example, as early as 1852, Horace Capron had come to Katumse's and Sanaco's Penateka (Southern Comanche) village near Camp Johnson on the Concho River and had found the Indians starving. The chiefs had complained to him bitterly. "What encouragement have we," one had asked, "to attempt the cultivation of the soil, or raising of cattle, so long as we have no permanent home? In every attempt we have ever made to raise crops, we have been driven from them by the encroachment of the white man before they could mature.

"Over this vast country, where for centuries our ancestors roamed in undisputed possession, free and happy, what have we left? The game, our main dependence is killed and driven off, and we are forced into the most sterile and barren portions of it to starve. We see nothing but extermination left for us, and we await the result with stolid indifference. Give us a country we can call our own, where we may bury our people in quiet."

Undoubtedly this had a touching appeal to the Texans of that time, as it had later for Lee. The Indians had been the victims of the white man's land hunger. But the federal government could not step in to help the Indians, for upon entering the Union in 1845 Texas had reserved all its public land. More than once Indian officials had asked the Texans to relieve the federal government's embarrassment by appropriating land for reservations; and at last on February 6, 1854, the state legislature had set aside for this purpose twelve leagues, to be located in not more than three tracts.

When Marcy and Neighbors, preparing to survey the reservation sites, procured a map from the Texas Land Office, they were surprised to find that much of the region they had expected to explore had already been claimed by land companies and individuals.

This was discouraging, but they proceeded with their work. They examined the sterile badlands and waterless region of the upper Colorado, Brazos, and Wichita rivers but found no sites suitable for their purpose. Next they turned to the valley of the Clear Fork, where finally they decided upon a tract of four Spanish leagues (17,712 acres), in the Camp Cooper country, for the Comanches. Then, near the junction of the Clear Fork and the Brazos, below Fort Belknap, they established another tract for the small bands of Caddoes, Anadarkos, Wacos, Tawakonies, and Tonkawas.

W. B. Parker, who accompanied Marcy and Neighbors on their journey, wrote a graphic narrative of their experiences in his *Unexplored Texas,* published about the time Lee came to Texas. He stated that on August 10, 1854, while the two dispirited men were returning to Fort Belknap, they were overtaken on the Clear Fork by Katumse, the Penateka chief, and two of his six wives.

Katumse was every inch an Indian leader, about fifty years old, six feet in height, with a dark red-bronze complexion. His striking physique, however, was offset by his ludicrous attire. He wore corduroy leggings and buckskin moccasins, an old, torn, greasy, checkered-cotton coat, and a "six-penny straw hat," while his horse's bridle "was ornamented with perhaps *fifty dollars worth of silver.*"

Parker described his wives as being hardly more than immature girls, one about eighteen and the other sixteen years old. The younger was chubby and dark; the older was lean, tall, and as fair as a quadroon. Their attire also bore the marks of long use. Both were dressed in dark calico shirts, with leggings and moccasins in one piece, like a boot. Their garments were dirty and common, and their heads were bare; their hair was short, thick, and uncombed. Parker thought that the younger was Katumse's favorite, for she had about her waist a wide belt studded with silver brooches, very heavy, showy, and costly.

Marcy entertained his red visitors at dinner. While they were eating, Sanaco's two subchiefs rode into camp, wearing umbrellas over their heads, much to the merriment of Marcy's party. The two Indians glared at the smirking Katumse and turned his self-satisfaction into furious anger when they denounced him to Marcy as a liar and scoundrel, with no authority to speak for the Penatekas. Only Sanaco had this right, they said. To prove this statement, they departed in search of him; and a few hours later they brought him in.

This rivalry for leadership of the tribe was of long standing. On August 21, 1853, Sanaco had addressed a lugubrious appeal to T. Howard and "to whom it may concern," asking for the censure of Katumse. He charged that his rival had urged the "commanding officer on the San Saba" to round up Sanaco and his band, and, if he would not mend his ways, to "fight me and kill me off."

While the subchiefs were away in search of Sanaco, at sundown Katumse visited Marcy's tent, holding in his hand a bundle of short stalks of grass. Seating himself before his host in dignified silence, he smoked his pipe for a few moments. Then he handed the stalks of grass, one by one, to Marcy, naming each as a chief or war captain of the Penatekas, and giving each one's attitude toward the whites. "After remarking upon four of high standing and three of mediocrity," Parker wrote, "he bundled the balance, eight in number, in a bundle, and handed them together, with a grunt and remark, 'No count!'" He affirmed solemnly that he alone could speak for the Penatekas and that he would accept in the name of his band whatever the Great Father in Washington had to offer.

The following morning Marcy's camp was pitched on the future site of Camp Cooper, near a spring and in a valley shaded by great elm and pecan trees, under which the Delaware scouts erected their lodges. Marcy arranged his wagons in a large semicircle, frontier fashion. Presently Sanaco led other bands to the valley, so that finally several hundred Indians had camped along the river.

Here, on August 20, Marcy opened his grand council with the Comanche chiefs and warriors. He told them that the Great Father at Washington had sent him to select a reservation for his red children, that they might have homes and learn to cultivate the soil and no longer pursue nomadic ways; for the buffalo and other game were fast disappearing, and shortly they and their people must resort to some means other than the chase for a living. Next, he warned the Indians bluntly that they must cease their depredations; if they did not, they would be hunted down and destroyed. The Great Father would not let them starve; he would send them agricultural implements and seeds and men to teach them how to farm; and he would give them food and clothing until they had grown their first crops. Marcy assured them that he knew of other Indians who had taken his advice and who now had plenty. If they did so, too, they would soon be free from want.

At this point in his narrative Parker had interwoven comedy with pathos. Katumse sat attentively as Marcy spoke, expecting to be called upon for a response. But without invitation Sanaco arose, ignoring the glowering displeasure of his rival.

"What I am about to say," he began, "will be straight-forward and the truth, and the sentiment of all my people. We remember what our former chief, Mo-ko-cho-pe, told us before he died, and we endeavor to carry out his wishes after he is gone. He visited our Great Father in Washington and brought us a talk from him. He told us to take the advice and example of the whites, and it would make us happy and benefit us.

"We are glad to hear the talk which has been sent us at this time; it makes our hearts warm, and we feel happy in knowing that our Great Father remembers his poor red children on the prairies.

"We accept this talk, and will endeavor to accede to all our Great Father requires of us." He then took his seat while his subchiefs nodded approval.

Katumse, frowning darkly, stalked away in silence when Marcy did not ask him to speak, too. But he was not too angry to rejoin his fellows a few moments later and accept some of the gifts which Marcy distributed. Eagerly men, women, and children crowded near. Printed cottons, handkerchiefs, blankets, knives, strouding for leggings, armlets of silver, and long wampum beads—all these were fabulous gifts beyond their wildest dreams. Then the council closed with another smoke, and Marcy invited the chiefs to dine with him.

At noon, under the great trees, the table was spread, and about it sat the expectant chiefs, who eyed hungrily the generous platters of bread, meat, and other good things until they were served. Yet they behaved "with great decorum," thought Parker, "using knives and forks, but wild Indian-like, never stopping until everything edible was consumed." Moreover, they returned for the next meal, and the next, until Marcy hinted broadly to them that his hospitality was exhausted.

Even then Katumse lingered, apparently still believing that Marcy would favor him over the other chiefs. But not so. Several hours later he came to the mess tent and asked the sergeant for corn and meat, only to be met by a rebuff. Then he and his wives mounted their horses and rode away, never once turning their heads to the right or the left or thanking their generous host for his hospitality.

While the chiefs were dining at Marcy's mess, beeves were slaughtered for the other Indians present. Marcy had also bought coffee, sugar, and corn for them at a near-by ranch. As soon as the beeves were killed, the Indian women began preparing them for immediate and future use. They consumed every extra edible part. Even the entrails, after they were slightly heated over the fire, were devoured while they were reeking with excrement.

They boned the flesh and then carved it into long slices, throwing them over poles to dry in the sun. "The caul, suet, and other inside fat, were dried whole, and the cannon bones and hoofs were first scorched before the fire and then hung up in the sun."

Those portions of meat intended for immediate consumption they placed upon a rude scaffold over a slow fire. This seared the meat, without depriving it of its juices, and prevented decomposition.

While the women were thus engaged, the warriors spent the day in gambling, in painting themselves and lounging about, or in wandering listlessly from lodge to lodge, expressing either surprise or pleasure by a grunt or a grin. They combed their hair in the middle, plaiting it in long queues and accentuating the divide across the head by a streak of yellow, white, or red clay. "A fat, chubby faced warrior," humorously wrote Parker, "painted a facsimile of a saw around his jaws in black, his cheeks red, his eye-lids white, and his forehead and divide of his hair yellow, smearing his body also with yellow." Another painted his face red, his eyelids white, and streaked his face with black, like a ribbed-nose babboon.

Katumse and Sanaco could not forget Marcy's food and gifts. He had promised other good things if they would accept Neighbors's reservation and raise corn, beans, and squash, like the Wichitas. Why should they not do this, they had asked themselves. Game had been driven away from its usual haunts and was increasingly hard to find. Every lodge was impoverished because of this scarcity—no skins for teepee covering and clothing and no food. If they returned to the Clear Fork, at least they would have temporary relief for their women and children. Hardly had the first frost of fall whitened the grass about their High Plains lodges before they broke camp, band after band, and started eastward.

When Neighbors rode up from San Antonio to the Clear Fork in November, 1854, he was surprised to find about 1,000 Penatekas—Katumse's, Sanaco's, and Buffalo Hump's—camped along the river above Fort Belknap. And hardly had he arrived before the chiefs came to him for a "talk." They urged him to hasten reservation arrangements, for their women and children needed food and a safe place to camp. Neighbors reassured them, stating that soon he would give them supplies and allow them to occupy the site Marcy and he had surveyed.

But presently the reservation plan met with near

disaster. During the preceding spring, while Marcy was yet in the Indian Territory, he had employed a Choctaw teamster, who joined the survey party in order to have the privilege of trading with the Indians. He had loaded his wagon with tobacco, knives, beads, calico, and wampum; but he found the Indians too poor for profitable trading. He learned, however, that other traders who had met with failure had found a way out. When the Comanches could offer nothing in exchange for their goods, they would wait until the Indians could procure horses and other plunder by raiding the border settlements. While this practice had kept the settlements in a ferment of excitement, nevertheless the stolen horses had enabled the Comanches to deal with the traders. In fact, while Neighbors was at Fort Belknap, angry settlers came to ask Major E. Steen, post commandant, to aid them in recovering some stolen horses. When Katumse and Sanaco learned of their mission, they volunteered to accompany Steen to Comanche villages between Fort Belknap and Fort Chadbourne on the Concho to assist in recovering the lost animals.

By the time that Steen and the two chiefs had arrived near Fort Chadbourne, however, one of Sanaco's warriors overtook them, bringing a German trader's warning to Sanaco. He was urged not to eat, sleep, or rest until he had broken camp and had taken his people out of danger of white soldiers, who were moving northward to destroy them. Katumse discredited the report, but Sanaco hastened back to his village and sent runners with the alarming news to other near-by bands, and within a day's time nearly all of them had scattered over the plains, going as far west as New Mexico and as far north as the Arkansas. Only 180 of Katumse's followers had remained to begin the reservation experiment.

Neighbors and Acting Agent Hill censured Washington army officials for ordering out the expedition that had caused the Indians so much alarm. Captain P. Calhoun had been sent out from Fort Chadbourne with a body of cavalry to hunt down raiding bands of Tanima and Nakoni Comanches, and was told to attack any band found near the border.[1] Calhoun's blunder had sadly imperiled the government's reservation program. "Half a million dollars," Hill wrote on February 11, 1855, "will not produce the same quiet and calm condition of the Indian mind that existed on this frontier forty days ago."

But, unfortunately, censure could not repair the damage done. Neither Buffalo Hump nor Sanaco would ever again risk bringing their bands to Camp Cooper. In the end this was fatal. With only a part of the Penatekas on the reservation, the government's policy could not succeed. Neighbors and his agents could not keep the wild Indians from using the reservation as a base for their raids on the border; nor could they restrain Katumse's warriors from occasionally joining their wild kinsmen.

John R. Baylor of Lagrange, Texas, was the first regular agent of Katumse's Comanches. Lee learned that when Baylor had first come to the Clear Fork to establish the reservation, he found that the initial 180 Indians had been increased to 277, all "wild, restless, and discontented." Baylor had employed conciliation, for he had only a small detachment of infantry to protect the agency, and

[1] This is only one of many similar instances where Indian agents and border army officers worked at cross-purposes.

34

LIEUTENANT COLONEL ROBERT E. LEE

with this small force he could not compel the Indians to remain on the reservation. Well mounted, they entered and left the reservation at will. He convinced Katumse, however, that he had all to gain and nothing to lose by remaining. Later, in January, 1856, with the arrival of the Second Cavalry, he could speak with more authority, and order began to appear out of chaos.

A few days later, Baylor called the Indians into council. He told them that the season was right to start farming. Already he had employed a farmer and a day laborer, and they had plowed 100 acres of land, which were now ready for planting. Pleased, Katumse and his warriors set to work with a will, planting corn, melons, beans, peas, and pumpkins.

When Katumse's prairie kinsmen learned of this, they also came in from time to time, so that when Lee arrived at Camp Cooper in April, 577 Indians had camped along the Clear Fork. Lee also caught the spirit and planted a garden to corn, cabbage, and other vegetables.

This was the state of the Texas reservation experiment that Lee found. At last the wandering Indians had been assigned homes under the watch of troops at Fort Belknap and Camp Cooper. And here at the latter post Lee was to serve as commandant.

Drought was another discouraging factor with which Lee and Katumse's people had to deal. The Indians should have read the Great Spirit's message written across the sky; but if they did, they said nothing about it. Lee, the newcomer, knew little about Texas weather. Day after day dust filled the air and norther followed strong southwestern winds. The wind was hot and parched the skin, leaves on the trees drooped, and spring clouds melted as though they were of snow. Lightning flashed and thunder boomed along the Clear Fork, but little rain fell. Black night clouds of April and May slipped around to the west or east, and morning dawned on dry land.

It was easy to convince Indians who had accepted the reservation only halfheartedly that the Great Spirit was angry. Day after day the sky was red with sand. Then came more positive proof. One morning shortly after their corn had put forth its tender shoots, the northern sky was darkened, but it was not a norther—it was grass-hoppers! And when these pests had finally moved on, they left a bare field. This was too much. The superstitious Indians abandoned all efforts to farm, and some joined the Yamparikas (Northern Comanches) on a buffalo hunt along the Arkansas. However, Katumse persuaded most of his people to remain. Even if their crops had failed, he reasoned, the Great Father in Washington would provide food and clothing for them.

Fortunately Lee did not witness the ravages of the drought on his garden. While his vegetables were yet green, he had led his cavalry in a patrol beyond the fron-tier.

Reconnaissance

DROUGHT appeared along the Clear Fork before May was far spent. Rain clouds piled up against the eastern sky like buttered popcorn but kept at a distance. Dry norther followed hot southwester. Often in the morning the sky was blue and smiling; but at midday, brassy and frowning. The water at the ford was a mere trickle; and even the branches of the widespread pecan and elm waved disconsolately in the wind.

Choking dust, blistering heat, spiders, ants, flies, loneliness, and deprivation—all these made Lee's early days at Camp Cooper hard to bear. Frustration weighed heavily on his sensitive soul. Good manners, broad learning, and military skill must have seemed of little use in a place like this. True, he could enjoy an occasional visit with an officer and his family, at luncheon, at dinner, or at a party; but these occasions afforded but temporary diversions. Always he thought anxiously about the welfare of Mary and his children. He wanted both his sons and his daughters to have the best of educational advantages, for which his income was hardly adequate.

At border posts only common necessities could be had. In March, just before leaving San Antonio for Fort Mason, he had instructed Lieutenant Charles Radziminski, his young Polish subaltern, to procure supplies which they would need on their long journey and after they had arrived at Camp Cooper. He had explained that his own needs were simple—"a boiled ham, hard bread, a bottle of molasses, and one of extract of coffee." However, he also added other things—a canvas tent, tables, camp chairs, crockery, and cooking utensils. He found that white crockery cost as much in San Antonio as French chinaware in Baltimore, but he purchased one dozen plates, four dishes, two vegetable plates, six cups and saucers, and tea and sugar pots. He did this, he explained, because he got "very tired of tin, when used constantly." He also employed a French handy man and cook, but later found him better at caring for horses than at preparing food.

A balanced diet was out of the question at Camp Cooper, but the invigorating climate made the plainest food almost desirable. The blue morning dawns, the crisp air, the pleasant smell of a mesquite fire and simmering coffee not only brought serenity to Lee's soul but whetted his appetite. Under such circumstances the cook's breakfast was satisfying. Dutch oven–cooked biscuits, steak, occasionally eggs, molasses or stewed peaches, and apples for breakfast, and boiled beef, potatoes, beans, canned fruit, and bread for luncheon, followed by about the same food for dinner, were repeated day after day. Occasionally butter, a chicken, and milk were bought at a near-by ranch to add variety, or fish caught from the river, but still Lee no doubt thought often of Virginia's "fleshpots."

But how could he expect other than simple fare? Transportation difficulties deprived the border soldier of luxuries. More than seven hundred government trains, each of five, ten, or twenty wagons, left San Antonio for the frontier posts to only ninety-two contract wagons—

all laden with quartermaster's stores, medical supplies, ordnance, and even forage for horses and mules, since there was hardly a fort less than fifty miles beyond the settlements. Supplies had to be freighted by slow stages and over rough roads and trails. No wonder contractors charged $4.50 per one hundred pounds for freight hauled from Indianola to Camp Cooper!

Yet there was a degree of domesticity about Lee's camp. Not only was his garden worked industriously, but he built a house for his hens. At night, while on the road from Fort Mason to Camp Cooper, he had allowed them to roost on top of his wagons, and now they had become quite domesticated. He wrote his daughter Mildred on April 28 how he had built their Camp Cooper home. "I planted four posts in the ground," he explained, "and bored holes in each three feet from the ground in which I inserted poles for the floor and around which were woven the branches that formed it." This was done to protect the hens from the snakes. Next he converted the coop into attractive nests, filling them with grass. In a letter written to Mrs. Lee about this same time he said, "This morning I found an egg at my tent door." And the hen was so tame that she hopped on his writing table while he was at work and upset his ink. But to Mildred he grieved that "My rattlesnake, my only pet, is dead. He grew sick and would not eat his frogs and died one night."

Rattlesnakes were everywhere as the warm spring days came. They crawled from crags and crannies of near-by cliffs down into the valley to dispute with the prairie dogs their home-ownership. And usually the complaisant rodents vacated to build other homes, going on the theory, no doubt, that *two* "is a crowd."

While Lee was occupied at routine tasks, on May 27 he received Special Order No. 64 from headquarters at San Antonio, directing him to lead an expedition against hostile Indians. Sanaco's Penatekas had recently joined the Tanimas and Naconies to plunder the border settlements, and border protests had poured into the office of Brigadier General Persifor Smith, the department commander. Smith ordered Lee to take two companies of the Second Cavalry from Fort Mason and two from Camp Cooper, totaling not more than 160 men, and to rendezvous them at or near Fort Chadbourne, one hundred miles distant. He was to consult with Special Agent Neighbors concerning where the hostile bands would likely be found and about furnishing him with Indian trailers from the Brazos Agency. There was to be no misunderstanding on this point, for it was of the utmost importance that the plans and purposes of the War and Interior Departments of the federal government coincide.

Camp Cooper was all agog. Both officers and men were eager to go, for this kind of service made life at a border post tolerable. Still, only two companies of cavalry could make the reconnaissance. The other two must remain as the garrison, to be assisted by a third company from Fort Chadbourne until Lee returned. Lee presently ended speculation by choosing the first squadron, consisting of Van Dorn's and O'Hara's companies.

Lively preparations now followed. Wagons were filled with supplies for the men and corn and oats for the horses. The best horses were chosen, saddles and equipment inspected, and guns cleaned and oiled. Lee was as eager to be off as his men were; but before leaving, he rode down to the Comanche Agency to confer with Neighbors, who

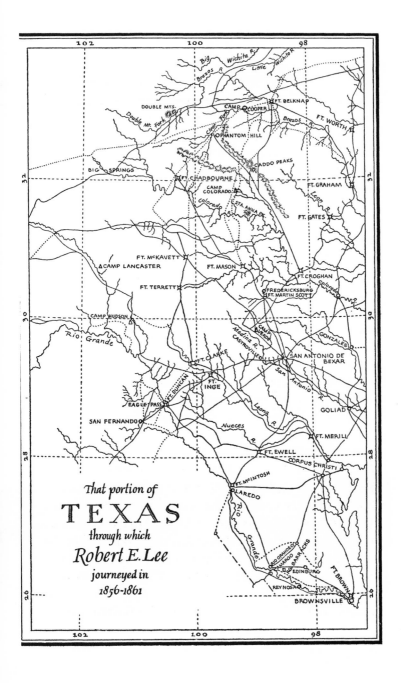

That portion of

TEXAS

through which

Robert E. Lee

journeyed in

1856-1861

received him courteously. The Agent told him where likely Indian camp sites could be found and how best to reach them. He also readily agreed for the celebrated Jim Shaw and his Delaware trailers to aid in the reconnaissance. No better guides were available. After the conference Lee rode back to Camp Cooper with deep respect for Neighbors, for he not only knew well the habits and problems of both the wild and the sedentary Indians, but was alert and progressive.

Lee knew that much importance was attached to this reconnaissance. Colonel Johnston had written Adjutant General Cooper: "I consider the movement of the Second Cavalry against the Indians absolutely necessary to the establishment of permanent security on the frontier." But both Johnston and the department commander had forgotten, if they ever knew, that at this time of the year the Southern Comanches generally joined their northern kinsmen on buffalo hunts in the Arkansas River country. Nevertheless, a band often lingered behind to steal horses, plunder from the settlers, and engage in illicit trade with the New Mexican *Comancheros*. And after all, these were the worst offenders.

Shortly after dawn Lee marched away with the first squadron of his command, the members of which were much envied by those left behind. With him were Jim Shaw and his Delawares. They traveled over the military road toward the southwest, over rolling hills, through mesquite valleys, across dry creeks and ravines, past the smut-scarred chimneys of old Phantom Hill, which had been abandoned as a military post and burned two years previously. From Phantom Hill the course was over rugged, broken hills and across a wide mesquite flat skirting

42

low-lying mountains thirty-five or forty miles distant. Castle Peak, standing as a lone vidette guarding Mountain Pass, could be seen thirty miles away, and it had served to mark the meandering road.

Dancing heat along the horizon did not dampen the ardor of Lee's men. Their column was imposing. First came Lee with Jim Shaw and the scouts; then followed the two companies of cavalry, with shining carbines and accoutrements; and finally, the heavily laden wagon train brought up the rear, with some of the teamsters riding and others walking.

Mountain Pass, about forty-five miles southwest of Phantom Hill, was a conspicuous landmark. The mountain rimming the plain here rose precipitously more than 250 feet and was sliced through by this deep gap. On either side its walls were covered with stunted bushes and boulders. In its trough ran a small brook fed by a spring, near which two years later a station was to be built on the overland stage road to California. Here Lee stopped and rested his command. Then he mounted to the tableland beyond the gap and continued his march over broken country to Fort Chadbourne, a short distance north of present-day Bronte, in Coke County.

The two companies of Fort Mason troopers under Captains Edmund K. Smith and William R. Bradfute had already arrived at Fort Chadbourne when Lee's column came in sight on June 17. A freight wagon laden with ammunition, bound for Camp Cooper, was also there; and from it, Lee supplied his men. About the post excitement and speculation were rife. Far to the south and west could be seen dense columns of smoke. Obviously, soldiers had not fired the prairies! Had suspicious Indians sent their warning signals to other bands of the coming of soldiers? Who else could have made them? If watchful Indians had set them off, Lee was told, the cavalry could be handicapped.

To prevent the news of his coming from spreading among those wild bands who might be camping west of Chadbourne, Lee hastily pushed out toward the Colorado River on the following morning. Twenty-five or thirty miles from the post his scouts brought him word that all the prairie south of the Colorado River was afire. Flames swept the dry grass with the speed of the wind, leaving the prairies black.

The cavalry struck the red-clay breaks of the Colorado on the fourth day out from Fort Chadbourne, and after crossing the river, moved on up its south bank for about twenty miles. The Delawares found several camp sites and trails, evidently made the previous spring by parties of Yamparikas (Northern Comanches) on their way southward to raid Mexican settlements. But there were no signs of recent occupation.

From the Colorado Lee's route turned northwestward, winding over hills and mesquite valleys until a high tableland was reached, across which ran Captain Randolph B. Marcy's wagon road of 1849. Back over this the troopers marched in a northeasterly direction. During better seasons these prairies were covered with grass and flowers, and the whir of wings and the call of quail, plover, curlew, and prairie chicken could be heard; but now, all life stood in silence while Nature brought forth her stillborn child, Drought. The day was hot, and mirages danced tantalizingly before the men, like limpid pools of fine water. But they did not complain. Presently they struck

44

the head of one of the tributaries of the Clear Fork and explored the region for an Indian camp but found none.

Lee now rode northward with his men, passing west of present-day Sweetwater, Roby, and Rotan. Searing heat continued to plague the men and horses. They found even the large creeks dry. Stagnant pools of briny or bitter water added to their misery, and their thirst went unquenched. Scouts sought out springs they had known in other seasons, but they, too, were dry. Since the troopers had to drink whatever water they found, many of them were stricken with diarrhea and dysentery. As the heat continued to climb above the hundred-degree mark, Lee's officers and men lost enthusiasm for their work. At last, on June 28, they crossed the Double Mountain Fork and made camp at the southern base of the two weather-beaten peaks, in present-day Stonewall County.

What Lee saw of the Double Mountains posed a vexing question. Undoubtedly in the past Indians had frequently camped and hunted through this country. But why would they frequent it at any time? As far as he could see to the east, there was a labyrinth of eroded hills, gulleys, and bare clay floors, except that here and there prickly pear, stunted mesquite, and cedar grew precariously. Some hills were capped by strata of sandstone, giving them the appearance of low-roofed houses. Briny pools, occasionally covered with green scum, were all the water that was left in the largest tributaries of the Double Mountain Fork; and the river itself was hardly more than a rivulet, its water brackish and muddy.

Game had abandoned the country, although old deer trails were everywhere. Only at night was there any evidence of life. As the men lay on their pallets, the coyote's howl, the owl's hoot, or the lobo's call to its mate broke the stillness.

But undoubtedly Indian videttes had frequently watched from the top of Double Mountains. Trails and camp sites, numerous but old, were all about. What Lee did not know was that in seasonable springs the region smiled with flowers, green grass, and pulsating life—a veritable Indian paradise. He only knew that it was now barren, that the grass was brown and crisp, and that the baked earth radiated heat so that his nights were far spent before southern breezes brought cool rest.

Lee spent three nights in his Double Mountains camp. For two days his troopers explored thoroughly the breaks, draws, and canyons, for twenty or thirty miles north, south, and west of the twin peaks. At the end of this time, he was forced to divide his command. Daily many of his troopers had weakened because of illness, and his horses had suffered from hard service and the terrific heat. Lee now ordered these sick men to mount the feebler horses and to conduct the wagon train south to the Clear Fork. And while they were moving southward, Captain Earl Van Dorn was to march at the head of the second squadron up the Double Mountain Fork to investigate a column of smoke seen rising in the distance. Scouts had come to Lee with the exciting news that they had discovered a fresh trail of a small Indian band. Lee had reasoned that if a small band were in the vicinity, then a larger one might be near; therefore, he was sending Van Dorn to investigate.

With the first squadron Lee turned down the river until he came to what he called its "north branch"; but he found no Indians. Then, with ten men from each company, he traveled northward, over a high plateau, until he came to the Little Wichita, following approximately the common boundary of Dickens and King counties. But again he met with disappointment—no Indians were found. At least he did find fresh water for the first time, and he and his men quenched their thirst and filled their canteens before they retraced their steps to the Double Mountains, where they spent their third night. On the succeeding morning they followed the tracks of the wagon train back to the Clear Fork.

Here on the Clear Fork, somewhere east of present-day Roby, Lee spent the Fourth of July. Some of his men were sick and others were tired, forlorn, and dispirited, for they had covered many fruitless miles. Prospects of adventure and new explorations had sent them forth; but they had found instead burning heat, a drought-stricken wilderness, fatigue, and illness. Later, in a letter to his wife, Lee expressed his feelings, as he could not do to his men. He said that he had spent the Fourth of July, after a march of thirty miles, on one of the branches of the Brazos, under his blanket, elevated on four sticks driven in the ground, as a sunshade. The sun was fiery hot, the atmosphere like the blast from a hot-air furnace, and the water salt. "Still," he concluded, "my feelings for my country were as ardent, my faith in her future as true, and my hopes for her advancement as unabated as if felt under more propitious circumstances."

Meanwhile, on June 29, Van Dorn moved out from his Double Mountains camp as Lee had instructed. Throughout the day his column marched westward along the river in the general direction from which the column of smoke had been seen that morning, while O'Hara and

47

his men followed along a parallel line about eight or ten miles farther back. Then at noon and again at sundown the smoke reappeared to the troopers' left. Van Dorn consulted with Jim Shaw, who was of the opinion that it was probably made by one band of Indians signaling to another. Since it was now sundown, Van Dorn decided to make camp and wait for the other two columns before attacking the Indians. With only the flickering campfire to give him light, he hastily penciled a message to O'Hara, stating his position. Then he sent out a Delaware scout with the letter; but the scout returned presently, saying that he had been unable to find the other men. Van Dorn then reported to Lee that the scout had failed because of stupidity or unwillingness to exert himself.

When daylight came, neither Lee nor O'Hara had arrived, and Van Dorn decided to proceed alone, screening his movements by following ravines and draws toward the signal smoke of the previous evening. By doing this, he presently came directly upon the camp of three Comanche warriors and a woman. Some of Van Dorn's men charged the camp, firing as they advanced, while others dashed between the Indians and their horses. Two of the warriors were killed, but a third succeeded in reaching his horse and rushing away. He was hotly pursued by Corporal Marshall, firing as he went. The fleeing Indian followed down a canyon, and when Marshall overhauled him, he leaped to the ground, ran through a cedar-covered area, and escaped.

Back at the camp, Van Dorn captured the woman, twelve horses, the Indian saddles, and supplies. O'Hara and his company, evidently hearing the firing, arrived on the scene just as the affray ended. Then O'Hara and Van

Dorn sent out small parties to reconnoiter the country for miles about the camp, but they presently returned to report that no other Indians had been found. The reunited troopers therefore retraced their steps to the Double Mountains, picked up the trail made by the wagon train, and followed it southward to the Clear Fork.

On the way to the Clear Fork the Indian woman told Van Dorn an interesting story. She first informed him that a fourth warrior had been out hunting at the time of the attack on the camp and had escaped. She stated also that they belonged to a Yamparika band residing north of the Arkansas; that four months earlier her party, including twelve warriors and herself, had gone to Mexico on a plundering expedition, in which they had been successful. On their way back they had been attacked north of the Rio Grande by white men and their booty taken; she with the four surviving warriors had escaped with nothing but the horses they rode. After traveling several days northward, they had stopped so that the warriors could raid the Texas settlements. Finally the men had returned with eight additional horses and some plunder. Then they had resumed their journey until they had come to the Big Springs of the Colorado, where they had stolen some cattle from a California train. These they had killed at their Double Mountain Fork camp, where they had stopped to rest, to eat a part of their beef, and to jerk enough of it for their journey back to the Arkansas, when Van Dorn attacked them.

When Van Dorn and O'Hara arrived at the Clear Fork, Lee was greatly chagrined to learn that he had missed the affray. While he was floundering through the Little Wichita breaks, Van Dorn had met and destroyed the only hostile Indian band the four companies were to find. Still, this small success served to renew his and the troopers' spirits.

He was particularly interested to learn that this Yamparika band had stopped at the Big Springs on their return from Mexico. While there several days past, his scouts had found well-beaten trails leading toward Mexico, apparently frequently traveled by raiding bands. If this were true, other bands might be there now. He therefore decided to return at once, even though some of his men were still sick and many of his horses were in poor condition. To alleviate the situation, he sent Lieutenant Walter H. Jenifer and twenty-seven troopers, including those sick men able to ride, on his feebler horses, as an escort for the wagon train, which was to move down the river via Chadbourne to the Concho.

With the remaining troopers Lee rode immediately to the Big Springs, but he found no fresh Indian trails. He now directed Van Dorn to march south to the headwaters of the Concho and to follow down its right bank to the Chadbourne-Mason road-crossing. Captain O'Hara was directed to move along the left bank. Lee himself was to go with Smith's company down the right bank of the Colorado, at the same time sending Bradfute and his company along the left bank. Each company was to keep in touch with the other and to report any suspicious signs of Indians.

Jenifer moved first with his wagon train early on the morning of July 9, Van Dorn and O'Hara that evening, and Lee with Smith and Bradfute the next morning. Seven days later they reunited at the Concho crossing without having seen any fresh signs of Indians but having

Military Plaza, San Antonio, about 1857

found the prairies south of the Colorado burned for a depth of thirty miles. Van Dorn came upon an Indian camp site near the headsprings of the Concho, probably occupied by Sanaco's band the previous spring, since the fire holes in the centers of the lodge sites still contained ashes. He also reported that a smaller band had visited the same region recently, and it was probably they who had fired the prairies.

Lee's force had found three other small camp sites which had probably been occupied by thieving bands the preceding spring. One was about fifteen miles below the Big Springs, the next about fifteen miles farther east, and the third about twelve miles above the crossing of the Chadbourne-Mason road. Each was located in a grove of willows or other trees and had not been occupied for at least a month, since near-by water holes were now dry.

At last the troopers turned homeward. Lee had made a determined effort to find any lurking raiders who might be within striking distance of the border settlements, but none could be found. His scouts told him that the Naconies, Tanimas, and Penatekas who had plundered the settlements during the past spring were now north of the Arkansas after buffalo. Lee was convinced that this was true and decided to return the four companies to their home posts. On July 18 he directed Smith and his company to descend the Concho to its mouth, cross to the San Saba, about the mouth of Brady's Creek, and ascend the valley of the San Saba to Fort Mason. Bradfute was to ascend Kickapoo Creek to the Spring, then cross to the San Saba and descend it on his route to Fort Mason. Both officers were to search for Indians on the way and to pursue them if they were found.

Lee followed with his first squadron, crossing the Colorado below Valley Creek. Then he passed east of Fort Chadbourne to the headwaters of Pecan Bayou, and thence on northward to Camp Cooper.

Camp Cooper was indeed a "haven in a weary land." The troopers had been absent for forty days. The separate columns had traversed eleven hundred miles of drought-stricken country and had found only uninhabited wastes, thirst, severe heat, and sickness—and a small band of Indians. They had brought back only a lone captive Indian woman, and when Lee learned that her father and mother lived on the Brazos reservation, he sent her to them without delay.

★ IV ★

Along the Rio Grande

THE Second Cavalry had been redistributed by
the time that Lee had returned from his recon-
naissance. Colonel Johnston had moved his headquarters to San Antonio, having succeeded Brevet Major
General Persifor F. Smith to the command of the department. Captains Van Dorn and O'Hara with their companies were to go from Camp Cooper to a point on the
Mason-Belknap road six miles from the Colorado River.
This would create a buffer zone between their camp and
Fort Mason and provide for a more elastic defense against
Indian raiders attacking the exposed Llano and Colorado
Valley settlements. Only Smith's and Bradfute's companies remained at Fort Mason. Captains James Oakes and
A. G. Brackett moved their companies to Fort Clark to
intercept marauding Comanches and Kiowas, who might
try to raid the north Mexican states. And to assist them,
Captain Innis N. Palmer's company was to be stationed
at Verde Creek and Captain Whiting's at a point where
the El Paso road crossed the Sabinal. Long since, the Mexican government had complained of these Indian raids,
and now Johnston proposed to do something about them.

But Lee had little time to think of troop changes;
other problems claimed his attention. The drought had
not yet run its course, and his troopers were in low spirits.

The Camp Cooper basin sweltered in oven-like heat, from which there was no relief, day or night; Lee's green garden of spring was now parched, and his "few cabbage and roasting ears had passed away." Those troopers, who on the recent expedition had drunk all kinds of water, "salt, sweet, bitter and brakish," had now the same experience at Camp Cooper.

Having to drink bad water, to endure intense heat, and to be without vegetables, the men were plagued by sickness; and Dr. John G. Gaenslen's hospital tent was crowded with patients, some afflicted with dysentery, some with scurvy, and others with more dangerous maladies. Lee visited his sick men regularly, rendering whatever aid and fatherly cheer he could. In spite of care some of those stricken died. Never did Lee demonstrate more devotion to his men. To him, it was stark tragedy for strong young men to die. On July 31 he stood by at the death of Lieutenant George M. Dick and later wrote the youth's father the sad news, saying that "inflamation of the intestines" had been the fatal ailment and that the Lieutenant had died calmly, whispering, "I am going to a better world." Lee buried him with military honors and masonic rites.

He was also worried because of his wife's illness at home. Several weeks earlier she had gone to a Virginia health resort but had recently returned home unimproved. Then, as if he were not enough burdened, he also received the sad news that his sister Mildred, Mrs. Edward Vernon Childe, had recently died in Paris. "I had never realized that she could have preceded me on the unexplored journey upon which we are all hastening," he wrote Mrs. Lee sorrowfully. "I pray that her life has just

begun, and I trust that our merciful God only so suddenly and early snatched her away because he then felt that
it was the fittest moment to take her to himself."

Fortunately, pressing military and social duties helped
to soften his grief. Hardly had he buried Lieutenant
Dick before Inspector General Joseph K. F. Mansfield
arrived at Camp Cooper. Lee erected a tent for him beside his own and set a plate for him at his table, for his
visitor was a distinguished Mexican War veteran. The
two men enjoyed recounting their campaign experiences
and talking of current problems. Lee accompanied Mansfield about the post, while the latter told him much about
Texas' military problem, its widely dispersed population,
its remote settlements, and its inadequate defense.

In turn, Lee told much about the Comanche reservation and the wild bands that yet roamed the prairies and
gave his guest expert opinion. Undoubtedly the Indian
agents also called on Mansfield to pay their respects, for
he later wrote that Neighbors was "a gentleman extremely well qualified" as supervising Indian agent, and that
under him S. P. Ross of the Brazos Agency and Baylor of
the Comanche Agency were "perfectly competent" and
"qualified" for their positions.

Ross had encouraged the "peaceful and harmless"
Brazos Indians to build permanent "log and grass huts
and houses . . . and to plant 700 acres of corn." Yet for the
second successive year drought had cut the yield to the
vanishing point, so that the Indians had been forced to
kill their own cattle and fowl to supplement their government rations.

On the other hand, the Inspector saw the Comanche
problem as Lee saw it. He noticed, of course, that Ka-

tumse's people had herds of horses and cattle, flocks of chickens, and 160 acres of drought-blighted corn; but he learned that only the women worked the fields, while the warriors engaged in hunting, occasionally joined raiding parties, or loafed about their village. Katumse's Mexican captives surprised him. His people had "among them 25 men and boys, and 15 women and girls as prisoners," he entered in his inspection report; and those who had become Indianized were "worse than the Indians in rascalities." Nevertheless, he felt that all the captives should be ransomed and returned to their Mexican homes.

Van Dorn and O'Hara had left with their troopers for their new station before Mansfield's arrival, and two companies of the First Infantry had taken their places at Camp Cooper. These were under Captains J. N. Caldwell and John H. King. Mansfield's report on the quality of both the officers and the men of the new companies was entirely favorable, since they were men seasoned in border experience.

He commended equally the Second Cavalry units, including Lee, the post commandant, despite the obvious faults of the camp. At best Camp Cooper was a tent post and without normal conveniences. Frequent trooper desertions resulted. Company K of the Second Cavalry had a total of forty-six absent without leave; and "extra-duty" men and those in the guardhouse swelled the number of malcontents.

For four days Lee and Mansfield looked in on Camp Cooper's every nook and cranny—the officers' quarters, the enlisted men's barracks, the hospital, the commissary, the arsenal, and even the horses' picket line (for there were no stables). Mansfield moved expertly from place to

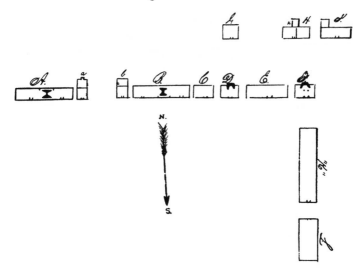

Second Lieutenant I. F. Minter's Drawing of Camp Cooper,
accompanying his Inspection report of
June 30, 1859

A: Barracks, Company D; mud walls with shingle roof.

B: Barracks, Regimental Band, Second Cavalry; same
construction.

C, D, F: Small buildings of rough stone and oak boards; *C*
used as Adjutant's office; *D,* Quartermaster and Commissary; *F,* storage.

E: Commissary storehouse; rough stone with shingle roof.

G, H: Built of pickets and rough boards; *G,* kitchen for
Commanding Officer; *H,* Regimental Quartermaster,
Second Cavalry.

I: Assistant Surgeon's quarters; rough stone and oak boards.

K: Temporary storehouse; tarpaulins on frames.

L: Temporary storehouse for forage; tarpaulins on frames.

a: Messroom and kitchen; pickets and oak boards.

b: Storeroom and saddler's shop; rough stone and oak boards.

k: Kitchen.

place, making suggestions here and nodding approval there. He and Lee watched target practice, in which the contestants fired at a mark one hundred yards away, and were surprised that the cavalrymen made better scores than the infantrymen.

At last, on August 4, inspection was completed, and Mansfield rode down the valley of the Clear Fork, bound for Fort Belknap, while Lee turned his attention to post duties.

Two weeks later, in midafternoon, Lieutenant Joseph H. McArthur and his family arrived. To Lee the border was no place for women, and his sympathy went out to Mrs. McArthur, a pretty, inexperienced, New York woman. She and her two small children had come with Lieutenant McArthur to make Camp Cooper their home. Lee feared that they did not understand the difficulties and trials of living at a border post and tried to help them adjust themselves to the conditions. For the first day he gave them his own tent, furnishing a narrow bed for the two children and a pallet for the Negro woman servant and her child. Later he erected two tents for the family on the bank of the Clear Fork. He gave the children bread and molasses to stay their hunger until supper and served their elders with water and wine.

It pleased Lee to act as a hospitable host, particularly in making Mrs. McArthur and the children feel that they were welcome. One can well believe that they reminded him of his own family two thousand miles away, for he was presently engaged in writing home. To his beloved Mary he expressed his concern about her illness, saying that he would trust a kind Providence to heal her. He urged that she impress on his children's minds the necessity of study. He wanted Rob to learn industry, thrift, and prudence, and to study Latin, French, arithmetic, and handwriting; if he learned these well, he would be fit for any task. But he advised against reading fiction because he thought it painted beauty more charming than nature and described happiness that did not exist. He urged his small daughter, "Life," or Mildred, to read and improve her mind: "Read history and works of truth— not novels and romances."

Then came urgent news. Lee's scouts had learned that Comanche raiders, Yamparikas, in small war parties of six, eight, and ten, after having ravaged the Mexican settlements, were trying to slip past Camp Cooper on their way back to the Arkansas by moving through the heavy timber farther east. This was proof of what Commissioner George W. Manypenny had recently said. "These bands who spend the winter below the Arkansas and commit depredations on the Texas frontier," he charged, "proceed northwardly in the spring in pursuit of buffalo. They are well supplied with horses, and enrich themselves by plunder. They receive their annuities on the Arkansas and regard them as compensation paid them by the United States for the use of the Santa Fe road by emigrants." (He probably had forgotten that they had been bribed not to attack the traders by Commissioners Arbuckle and Stokes at Camp Holmes in 1835.) "Like the Kiowas," he concluded, "they are insolent, and treat their agent with contempt." If this were true, thought Lee, he would teach them a much-needed lesson. Quickly he made plans to pursue them with a troop of cavalry supplied for a twenty days' expedition, but other factors intervened, and the expedition did not go out.

As the summer wore on, the heat increased. But at last, in late August, cooling rains fell on a thirsty earth. Not once but twice downpours drenched the valley. And again thunder boomed and rolled down the river, and lightning snapped and crackled among the trees. Then the sleeping Clear Fork awoke and roared its delight, the water at the ford rising to the girth of the cavalry horses. The gentle patter of rain on canvas was music to the listening troopers, who breathed deep into their lungs the sweet smell of rain on the parched land. But most welcome was the cool wind which blew steadily from the east following the heavy rain and which drove away the dancing heat. Again grass and flowers brightened the landscape, and even the birds seemed to welcome the change.

Such a temporal blessing caused Lee to think of God's goodness. "We are all in the hands of a kind God who will do for us what is best," he wrote Mrs. Lee, "and more than we deserve. . . . May we all deserve his mercy, his care and his protection."

But he wrote reproof for those who were pressing his claims for a brigadier generalship. Of course he was vitally interested in promotion, but he wanted those in authority to recognize his merits without pressure. His Virginia friends had felt that President Franklin K. Pierce might forget him while he was stationed on the frontier and had addressed a petition to him in Lee's behalf. They reminded the President that Lee had graduated from West Point "with the highest honors," and that he deserved reward for his "life long services in peace and war, his brilliant and pre-eminent distinctions won upon the field," and for other things. If a brigadier generalship were to be created, they asked that it be given to Lee. But Lee gently chided Mrs. Lee and her father for encouraging the petition. "If it is on my account that you feel an interest in it," he wrote, "I beg you will discard it from your thoughts. You will be sure to be disappointed. Nor is it right to indulge in improper and useless hopes. It besides looks like presumption to expect it."

Lee's Virginia friends were right in believing that official Washington sometimes forgot border officers. It was equally true that the dreariness of post life, with only occasional reconnaissances, purposeless drill, and court-martial sessions, smothered their ambitions and threw them into a rut. Lee constantly sought variety, but again and again frustration beset him. Just now his proposed Indian campaign promised a change. Then his plans were wrecked by the arrival of a courier bringing him a summons for a court-martial session at Ringgold Barracks. He was to sit in trial of an old friend, Major Giles Porter. At once he began preparations for his long journey, writing to Mrs. Lee that he would be gone two and one-half or three months and that at Fort Mason Major Thomas would join him as a traveling companion. Lee had a marked fondness for this fellow Virginian, a calm and silent man, shy and modest as a maiden, with silver-blue eyes that flashed only under emotion—"Old Slow Trot" Thomas.

On September 2 Lee and his small escort left Camp Cooper. They rode down the river until they came to "Samboheads," then turned toward the Mason road. Twenty-seven miles out they crossed "the three creeks" and encamped for the night on the last one. Up to this point their journey had been pleasant; the day was cool and vegetation showed green from the recent rain. But after supper a terrible rainstorm broke and raged all night, so that, when morning came, the brooks and ravines were filled with water. And when they came to Hubbard's Creek, it, too, was a roaring torrent; and they had to spend the remainder of the day on its bank. From here they rode down the Fort Mason road through Shackelford and Coleman counties, past West and East Caddo Peaks and through heavily timbered country to Camp Colorado. Here they made only a brief stop. They crossed Jim Ned's Creek and continued southward, passing on their left the imposing Santa Anna peaks rising from a mesquite plateau like two huge apartment houses. Then they crossed the Colorado and entered a beautiful hill country, in the deep valleys of which were limpid streams, such as the spring-fed Brady's Creek and the San Saba River. On September 8 they arrived at Fort Mason, 165 miles from Camp Cooper. Here Lee and Thomas loaded their baggage and camp equipment into a wagon and united their escorts and mess.

Promptly at eight o'clock the next morning they started for San Antonio, the next stop on their journey, making halts at the German towns of Fredericksburg and Boerne. On their third day out from Fort Mason they reached San Antonio and were joined by one of Lee's friends of West Point days, Captain James A. J. Bradford. However, Lee could not forget domestic problems, and while at San Antonio he wrote Mary that he was greatly concerned because of her illness. "I pray that he [God] may relieve you in his own time."

On September 13 the travelers reached the quaint Alsatian town of Castroville, a replica of the poor villages of the Rhone Valley of France. It was settled by French and Germans as the result of a colonial grant made to Henri Castro, of Portuguese descent, by the congress of the Texas Republic, on February 15, 1842. It was a thriving place for the border, with a good mill, stores, and tile-roofed cottages scattered prettily. Lee found the M. Tardé Hotel a two-story house, with double galleries, "the best tavern in Texas." Here the weary travelers had not only white bread, sweetmeats, and potatoes, but napkins, silver forks, and radishes, French servants, French neatness, French furniture, delicious French beds, and the "lively and entertaining bourgeoise."

Lee's party was now traveling across Medina County over the Eagle Pass road, through a beautiful live-oak region, the deep shade of the oak relieved here and there by the yellow-green of the mesquite. Twenty-five miles farther along the road they reached D'Hannis, "like one of the smallest and meanest of European peasant hamlets." It consisted of about twenty cottages and hovels, all built of jacal (upright poles with their interstices made tight with clay mortar), the floors of beaten earth, the windows without glass, the roofs built so as to overhang the siding and covered with a fine, brown grass thatch, the ridge line and apexes being ornamented with knots, tufts, crosses, or weathercocks. This was a second colony established by Castro in 1846.

Lee found this town interesting also, but he and his friends did not stop. They crossed the Frio River farther along the road and arrived at Fort Inge on the Leona River in Uvalde County at ten o'clock on the morning of September 16. As was usually the case with border forts, there were no structures for defense, except a stockade of mesquite logs about the stables, which were open, thatched sheds. The post consisted of about a dozen buildings of various sizes, officers' quarters, barracks, a bakery, a hospital, a guardroom, and others, all scattered about the border of a parade ground, pleasantly shaded by hackberries and elms. The buildings were rough and temporary, some of the officers' lodgings being jacal. But all were whitewashed and neatly kept, by taste and discipline. Captain Whiting of the Second Cavalry, with Company K, had only recently arrived to take command of this post, and both he and his men gave Lee and his fellow travelers a hearty welcome.

From this point on to Fort Duncan on the Rio Grande, about fifty miles to the southwest, the country was desolate. There was "no grass for the horses or shade for the men." Lee described it as a "wretched country, no trees, or grass, cactus; thorny acacia are the only growth." The road was rough, and there were water holes and ravines everywhere, but no water.

This was Indian country. Only a short time prior to Lee's coming, a sergeant who was bringing a load of hay into Fort Duncan was pounced upon by a band of Indians, within a mile of the post, and before his men could deploy to meet the attack, "their mules were cut from the traces under his nose, and jerked into the chaparral."

Fort Duncan was reached at midday on September 18, and Lee and his friends found food and water and rest from travel and the fiery sun. Fort Duncan was a more important post than Fort Inge. A fine band played upon the terrace at the close of evening and fashionably dressed ladies added pleasing domesticity to so remote a place.

But the row on row of brown-topped sheds, cabins,

military storehouses, and blocks of white tents showing through a bright green mesquite grove were in sharp contrast to the wretched-looking Mexican hovels of Piedras Negras beyond the sluggish Rio Grande, or to those of Eagle Pass, above the fort and on the American side of the river. Upon approaching the town from Fort Duncan, a visitor could see a few tottering shanties, mere confused piles of poles, brushwood, and rushes, with hides hung over the doors; broken cart wheels, yokes, and other rubbish; chickens were running loose, and hogs were sleeping in holes they had rooted out on the shady sides. Most noticeable of all were two or three adobe houses, looking like long, two-story sepulchres, but which were used as stores. The population of the town was only two or three hundred people, the majority of whom were Mexicans.

From Fort Duncan Lee had expected to travel through wild and lonely country to Laredo, his next stop, almost one hundred miles distant, and quite unoccupied except for a few ranchers, Mexican outlaws, and wild animals. In his "Memo Book" he listed "Rattlesnake Den and Turkey Creek" as two of his stopping places, but he also must have crossed Cuevas, Cuero, and Abrasta creeks and Arroyo de los Hermanos, if he traveled the Duncan-Ringgold Barracks military road paralleling the Rio Grande. He had also expected dry, warm weather, such as he had encountered between Forts Inge and Duncan, but he was agreeably surprised. A short distance from Fort Duncan he rode into a rainstorm, and his journey for the remainder of the way was pleasant, with only one exception.

A swollen stream detained the party for one day. The men finally decided that it was safe to cross and swam their mules and floated the wagon over. But water came

up into the wagon bed and wet Lee's wardrobe thoroughly, from his socks to his plume. They were "immersed in
the muddy water—epaulets, sash, etc.," he wrote Mrs.
Lee ruefully; then he added, "They are, however, all dry
now." Lee's mare took him over the stream comfortably.

Continuing down the Rio Grande, on the sixth day
out from Fort Duncan, Lee and Thomas overtook Colonels Bainbridge, Seawell, and Bumford, also going to
Ringgold Barracks to attend the trial. This gave them
much pleasure, for they had seen few travelers along the
way. The combined party now resumed its journey, passing through Zapata and Starr counties, and arrived at
Ringgold Barracks, just below Rio Grande City, on Sunday, September 28. Lee and Thomas encamped outside
the garrison since no other acceptable quarters were available. Lee had good cause to feel tired; he had been in
the saddle for twenty-seven consecutive days and had
covered 730 miles since leaving Camp Cooper.

Lee was favorably impressed with his brother officers
who, with him, composed the court. "Captain Bradford
whom we knew at Old Point (Virginia) is on the court,"
he wrote Mary. And others were "Colonel Chapman of
the Infantry, from Georgetown, Captain Marcy [Ran-
dolph B. Marcy], Colonel Bainbridge, Bumford, Ruggles,
and Seawell, and Captain Sibley, an old Classmate of
mine. Colonel [Carlos A.] Waite is president of the court
and Captain Samuel Jones, of the Artillery, judge advocate." He added that Jones had brought his wife and
child with him in a six-mule road wagon from Sinda,
about 120 miles up the Rio Grande. In concluding his
letter, Lee apologized for his cramped writing. His finger
was stiff, "caused by a puncture from a Spanish bayonet

GENERAL GEORGE H. THOMAS

while pitching my tent on the road, which struck the joint." This accident probably caused Lee to feel that Colonel Jones had made a mistake in bringing his family with him. "Every branch and leaf of this country," he wrote, "are armed with a point, and some seem to poison the flesh. What a blessed thing the children are not here. They would be ruined."

He again wrote two weeks later, saying that the trial was under way but that it progressed slowly. He could not see its probable end. Five of the officers of the court were assigned with troops for Florida service and were impatient to get away. Mrs. Waite was packing. The Waites had no children and had good servants and a very convenient carriage. They also had camp furniture made for quick putting up, taking down, and carrying about. He presumed that Mrs. Waite would have to leave her chickens, goats, and pigeon. Then humorously he added: "If officers of the army will get married, I think they should insist that their wives have no children. This will help the matter much." Already he had made friends with Colonel Sibley's two small children, a girl and a boy. "I have become very intimate with them," he wrote lightly. "They would be willing to go with me to Camp Cooper if their mother would permit."

Lee found time dragging on his hands at Ringgold Barracks. Major Porter had employed two Texas lawyers, a Judge Bigelow and a Colonel Bowers, to represent him. They were very shrewd attorneys, accustomed to the tricks and stratagems of special pleading, which, Lee thought, "if of no other avail, absorb time and stave off the question." But this gave him added leisure for letter writing. Earlier he had written Agnes about Camp

Cooper, his "Texas Home," its inconveniences and loneliness, and he had asked her to visit him. In reply she said:
"I am much obliged for your description of your camp.
. . . I know exactly what to expect if I go out there, but
I don't see that you have room for any additions to your
family, with your present accommodations." Still, she
admitted that she would like to live in Texas for a year
or two.

Then on October 24 Lee expressed to his wife his im-
patience because of the dragging court session. Those
officers who had been assigned to Florida stations were
eager to get away, he said, but the actual troop movements would not come until November 1. Nevertheless,
they were packing, and some were selling their surplus
beds, chairs, cows, goats, and chickens. "I am sorry to see
their little comforts going," he wrote, "for it is difficult
on the frontier to collect them again." Mrs. Sibley told
Lee that her chairs and cow had gone, and Mrs. Waite,
her goats. He was also concerned about Johnson, his handy
man and cook, who had fever. He hoped that it would
prove a slight case "for his sake and my own," he said,
"for though he is a poor cook, he is all I have, and neither
the Major [Thomas] nor I can stand these long and interesting sessions of the court without eating."

V

From Pillar to Post

MORE and more the greatness of Texas impressed Lee. Its rolling hills and valleys, its sparkling rivers and fine forests, its vast farms and ranches, its diversified climate, and its friendly, hospitable people affected him strongly, while the spirit of optimism which he observed in the state was unlike anything he had seen or felt elsewhere. At first this annoyed, then puzzled him, then led him to understanding and admiration. And as appreciation of this attitude came to him, he could ride along extended trails and view wide-sweeping prairies and semiarid wastes without feeling too lonely; he could camp among ever present dangers, far removed from human habitation, without fear, and find peace. His letters home at this time reveal the spiritual change that was taking place within him, a change that was almost imperceptible but nevertheless real, one that increased his strength, poise, and dignity. Brother officers who witnessed his metamorphosis stood in awe and respected him, though they could not enter into intimate friendship with him. None felt that he could call him "Bob" or in any way establish familiar relations. Yet each knew, also, that he could go to him with any problem, however personal, and find a sympathetic listener and friend, whose advice would be sound, for when Lee spoke, all took heed to his counsel.

This mental and spiritual adaptation made the stay at Ringgold Barracks less an ordeal for Lee than for his brother officers. Day after day the shrewd Texas lawyers engaged in verbal clashes with Judge Advocate Jones, dragging out the trial through October. Members of the court became restless and gave vent to heated argument and quarreling, with Lee counseling peace. Finally, on November 1, the trial was transferred to Fort Brown, near the mouth of the Rio Grande. Promptly Lee and Thomas struck their tent and turned it and their wagon and six mules over to the Ringgold Barracks quartermaster until they could start their journey home. Lee paid his servant Johnson his wages and left him in the hospital, and then ordered Corporal McCarty to take his detail of men to Commandant Ricketts of the post for a temporary assignment. Then he and Thomas boarded the steamer *Ranchero* for Brownsville. When they reached Fort Brown on November 3, they occupied a room at the officers' quarters with young Lieutenant Howard, engaged their meals at Victor's Restaurant, and made themselves as comfortable as possible for whatever period might be necessary for the trial, which was resumed on the next day.

But the end of the trial was not in sight. Judge Advocate Jones heatedly pressed his charges; and, in turn, Judge Bigelow and Colonel Bowers defended their client with vigor. Once again members of the jury, tired and fretful, joined in the bickering, much to Lee's annoyance.

Brownsville was like many another border town, with its progressive, better-class people and its flotsam and jetsam of both Mexico and the United States, including shiftless *peones* thronging the streets on Saturdays and

Sundays. Lee wondered why army officers would bring their wives and families to such an out-of-the-way place. "The more I see of Texas army life," he wrote his wife on November 19, "the less probability do I see of you ever being able to join me here. Our family is too large and unwieldy to commence campaigning." Perhaps his own cramped quarters suggested this thought. He made his pallet in one corner of the room, Howard in another, and Thomas in another. He sympathized with Lieutenant Howard's young wife, who was now having a foretaste of army life while living with her sister's family in Brownsville. Lee called on her and assured her that this experience was not typical of what she could expect. Soon young Howard would be transferred to Fort Leavenworth, where she would have better accommodations and a chance to meet other persons of her own age and sex. She presently bade Lee good-by, hopeful of the future.

Once more frustration pressed in on Lee's sensitive soul as the court-martial dragged out its weary length. One day was much like another—the assembling of the court, the testimony of witnesses, pointless bickering, adjournment, and long hours of waiting for the next day.

To relieve the tedium, Lee sought the society of friends, but they helped him through only a part of the day. Then on Sunday he attended church twice, but the minister was colorless and almost read his sermons, and he was not even a good reader.

Lee found interest in long walks or rides away from the post, studying the plant life of the country; or he engaged in the pleasurable task of writing to members of his family. What were they doing? Was Mary's health improved? Were she and the children comfortably supported? Did his children have the proper educational advantages? These questions gave him most anxious concern. And his several letters reveal that he not only thought of his family but prayed for them daily, for Lee was a devout man.

Then his love for his state and his nation profoundly moved him, as is seen in a letter to Mary on December 13. He expressed a hope that President-elect James Buchanan of Pennsylvania would be able to "extinguish fanaticism, north and south, and cultivate love for the country and the Union, and restore harmony between the different sections." He found much interest, too, in the Alexandria *Gazette*. It gave him not only the local news but also the trend of Virginia politics and the thinking of prominent men on the state's economic, political, and social problems. If absence does make the heart grow fonder, Lee's love for his state deepened during these long hours of introspection, while living on the Texas border. The ominous slavery controversy, waxing increasingly dangerous to the peace of the nation, filled him with foreboding. If secession should come, what would Virginia do? Being adjacent to the federal capital would place her near the vortex of sectional discord. Fortunately, however, there were local distractions which kept Lee from worrying too much about these things.

Not the least of them was the weather. Midsummer heat was frequently followed by a sharp norther. On December 19 Lee took one of his customary walks away from the post. The weather was so warm that he had worn a summer coat. For a time his attention was given wholly to his surroundings as he followed a path through the chaparral. The landscape was bright with flowers. At one place he noticed an althea with a crimson blossom like a red rosebud, and everywhere were wild verbenas with rich orange and red petals. While enjoying these sights, about sunset he was caught in a rainstorm and turned back in his walk. Scarcely had he reached the fort, wet to the skin, before a norther sprang up; and all his blankets could not keep him warm. The following morning he wrote Mary: "This morning great coats are necessary. The Norther still rages and flakes of snow fill the atmosphere."

But this diversion from worry was temporary. A steamer had just arrived at Brownsville from New Orleans, bringing a "full file of papers," which Lee read with interest. Among the items of national consequence, he endorsed President-elect Buchanan's policy toward slavery, a policy that neither pleased Northern abolitionists nor Southern "firebrands." Lee felt that the abolitionists must be aware that their activities were unlawful and that moral suasion was preferable. Negroes were better off, he thought, than they would be in Africa; and as to their enslavement, only a "merciful Providence" could determine its length. He believed that their freedom would come eventually through the "mild and melting influence of Christianity." Why couldn't abolitionists see this? "The doctrines and miracles of our Savior," he said, "have required nearly two thousand years to convert but a small part of the human race." Why should the abolitionists expect to accomplish similar results by violent, immediate means? "We must leave final emancipation to Him who chooses to work by slow influences," he reasoned. As he grappled with the problem, more and more he became certain that the abolitionists were the untiring agitators of sectional discord. "Is it not strange," he asked, "that descendants of those Pilgrim fathers who crossed the Atlantic to pursue their own freedom of opinion, have always proved themselves intolerant of the spiritual liberty of others?"

That Lee also read with great interest the copies of the Alexandria *Gazette* from November 20 to December 8, which he had just received, is important to remember. For the first time he seemed to realize that his profound love for Virginia might ultimately clash with his near-instinctive love for the Union. What would he do if secession came? With much time on his hands, Lee had occasion to read and to think dispassionately. Sectional issues disturbed him. How could the nation survive such bitter strife? Only by the help of God, "who sees the end and who chooses to work by slow things."

On Saturday before Christmas Lee visited Matamoros, across the Rio Grande from Brownsville. He found the town neat, "though much out at the elbow," and apparently nothing of interest going on. The public square was inclosed, and the trees and grass flourished, largely because of the forethought of Major William Chapman of the Quartermaster's Department, who had made the improvement in 1846 while the town was occupied by the United States Army. The most attractive sights to Lee were the orange trees loaded with unripe fruit, the oleander in full bloom, and large date, fig, and palm trees.

Lee was lonely; Christmas was approaching. "My heart will be in the midst of you," he wrote Mary, "and I shall enjoy in imagination and memory all that is going on. May nothing occur to mar or cloud the family fireside, and may each be able to look back with pride and pleasure at their deeds of the past year and with confidence and hope to that in prospect." On his daily walks he visited near-by stores and managed to find presents for all the children—handsome French teapots, a beautiful Dutch doll, a "crying baby that can open and shut its eyes" for the girls; and knives and books for the boys. Then on Sunday Lee and Thomas went to church and afterwards dined with the clergyman, Reverend Passmore, on roast turkey and plum pudding.

Lee must have studied Proverbs, for in more than one letter to Mary and the children his advice was biblical. "You must study to be frank with the world," he wrote his small son. "Frankness is the child of honesty and courage. Say just what you mean to do on every occasion, and take it for granted that you mean to do right. . . . Never do a wrong thing to make a friend or to keep one. . . . Above all, do not appear to others what you are not. . . . We should live, act and say nothing to the injury of any one." And a short time later, he advised Mary: "Do not worry yourself about things you cannot help. . . . Lay nothing too much to heart. Desire nothing too eagerly, nor think that all things can be perfectly accomplished according to our own notions."

Earlier, while on his way from Ringgold Barracks to Fort Brown, Lee had formed a friendship with Captain King of the *Ranchero;* and while in Brownsville he called on Mrs. King. The King cottage was removed from the street by well-kept trees and shrubbery in the yard, among which were several orange trees filled with ripening fruit. Mrs. King's table was loaded with sweet oranges and many other things tempting to the eye, but, Lee wrote his wife, "I tasted nothing." He came for a short, formal call on Mrs. King, much to the dissatisfaction of several brother officers who went with him. They told him that on other occasions they had been entertained elaborately in other homes—cold meats, coffee, tea, fruits, and sweets! But Lee felt that to stay for dinner would violate social propriety.

Porter's trial lasted through January and until February 18, adjourning from day to day to await the appearance of the defendant's witnesses. Neither Lee's correspondence nor available official papers reveal just what the charges were, although the officers supported the defendant. A final angry debate arose over Judge Advocate Jones's announcement that he had forwarded to department headquarters a paper setting forth certain reasons why in his opinion the court should not have waited for witnesses—a paper that had already been rejected by the court. President Waite of the court was particularly harsh in his remarks. Lee regretted the whole circumstance, but within an hour after the adjournment of the trial sine die, he, Thomas, and other members of the court boarded the *Ranchero* for Ringgold Barracks.

At Ringgold Barracks the party divided, but Colonel Seawell, Major Thomas, and Captains Bradford and Marcy went on to San Antonio with Lee, as soon as he had recovered his escort, mules, wagon, and supplies. They followed the outer road to Fort McIntosh. They traveled for about forty miles almost due northward, through Starr County; then they turned northwestward, crossing Zapata and Encinal counties, through a densely overgrown chaparral region, before they reached Fort McIntosh.

Just before they struck the chaparral wilderness, they came to the favorite resort of wild horses, as well as deer, antelope, and other game. This was also the favorite resort of "mustangers," or wild-horse (mustang) hunters, whose business it was to recruit the stock of both Texans and Mexicans. While their ostensible purpose was to catch wild horses, a contemporary states that they often also practiced highway robbery, and were, in fact, prairie pirates, seizing any property that came their way, murdering travelers, and pillaging border trains and villages. Often they carried out these operations under the guise of Indians, and, at the scene of a murder, some "Indian sign," such as an arrowhead or a moccasin, was left behind to mislead justice.

Mustanger camps caught not only shady characters and notorious killers but men of several nations. Theirs was a dangerous profession, and it was only men of adventurous or devil-may-care spirits who found it interesting. Here and there they established their ranches as temporary homes or retreats, and generally near the known haunts of the wild horses.

The mustangs were degenerates of several breeds, some tracing their equine lineage back to the early Spanish Barb or Arabian (Moorish) steed. Occasionally one or more fine animals were found in the herds, but generally they were narrow chested, weak in the haunches, of bad disposition, and worth about one-tenth the price of improved stock. They were as wild as the buffaloes and much more dangerous, fighting viciously with their hoofs and teeth anyone who sought to capture them.

But the hunters took every precaution. They drove them between diverging and hidden wings into a pen.

Then they lassoed the mares and turned loose or shot those stallions that could not be tamed. Those which were tamed to be driven sold, delivered at the settlements, at eight to fifteen dollars per head. Only experienced horsemen bought them, so well known was their propensity for wildness. The settler believed that a mustang would "suddenly jump upon you, and stamp you in pieces, his vengeance all the hotter for delay."

When Lee and his friends reached San Antonio Wells, they found camped near by eight or ten bearded and desperate-looking mustangers. Lee did not encourage intimacy, but he watched them chase and capture about twenty colts. And at Las Animas, a short distance farther along his road, he watched twelve others lasso a roan mare, but he was more impressed with a beautiful iron-gray mare about four years old in the herd.

Lee's party did not tarry at Fort McIntosh, which they reached on March 6, but took a direct road to San Antonio, traveling over terrain as dry and rugged as that between San Antonio and Fort Duncan which Lee had traversed on his way down to Ringgold Barracks. The remainder of the journey was uneventful, and the weary travelers reached San Antonio on March 6, 1857.

Here Lee expected to find friends and a short rest before he resumed his journey to Camp Cooper, but a cruel disappointment awaited him. He must attend another court-martial, this time at Indianola. By now he was inured to such disappointment, and ten days later he started for his new assignment, having already ordered Thomas back to Camp Cooper. On this trip he traveled by stage, passing Gonzales and Port Lavaca en route. When he reached Indianola two days later, he lodged at the Cassimir House and prepared to make the best of his situation. Fortunately, this court, too, adjourned sine die, on March 28, and presently he was back in San Antonio.

Through all these trying experiences Lee remained in good spirits. While in Indianola he wrote his little daughter, Mildred, about cats. "You must be a great personage now—sixty pounds," he began. "I want to see you so much. Can you not pack up and come out to the Comanche country? I would get you such a fine cat you would never look at 'Tom' again." Then he told of the death of Jim Nooks, Mrs. Waite's cat. "He died of apoplexy," Lee teased. "I foretold his end. Coffee and cream for breakfast, pound cake for lunch, turtle and oysters for dinner, buttered toast for tea, and Mexican rats, taken raw, for supper. He grew enormously and ended in a spasm. His beauty could not save him." Then he told of other cats he had seen on his Rio Grande trip, one of which he would take back to Camp Cooper, if he could persuade the driver to give him a place on the stage. The cat belonged to a French woman, a Mrs. Monod. He was uncertain whether madame would trust her pet to go "into such a barbarous country and Indian society." The most unusual specimen he had seen was a wildcat. A Mexican had caught him near Fort Brown and was carrying him wrapped up in his coat when Lee met him on one of his walks. He offered to buy him, but the Mexican said that he was already sold. "I left the wildcat on the Rio Grande," Lee wrote. "He was too savage; had grown as large as a small-sized dog; had to be caged, and would strike at anything that came within his reach."

Back in San Antonio Lee could at last relax for a few

hours. The first night after his arrival, while he was camping near the town, a norther had blown up, and next morning Lee found a bucket of water in his tent frozen hard. As the weather was still cold and raw, he decided to remain in San Antonio until the norther had abated, especially since it was Sunday. When Lee's friends learned of his delay in leaving, they besieged him with invitations. He had supper with Colonel and Mrs. Johnston, and breakfast and dinner with Major and Mrs. Thomas. "The supper last night was so good," he wrote Mary, "and so much to my taste, venison steak, biscuit and butter, that I had little appetite for my breakfast, though waffles, eggs and wild turkey were three dishes that it presented; and when the dinner of wild turkey, tomatoes, French peas, snap beans, and potatoes was followed by plum pudding, jellies and preserved peaches, I despaired of eating any of Mrs. Smith's supper."

Before leaving for Camp Cooper, Lee saw one of Major Henry C. Wayne's camel experiments. Thirty-two of these hardy animals had been imported from the Mediterranean. Secretary of War Jefferson Davis had permitted their purchase to solve the transportation problem in the semiarid Southwest, and in 1856 a place for them had been established at Camp Verde, a short distance out of San Antonio. Lee had already seen a second caravan of forty-three camels, also purchased in the Mediterranean area, come into San Antonio under the care of their native tenders, and was quite amazed to see one of the animals rise from the ground "packed with two bales of cotton."

But just now he had little time to look further into this interesting experiment. As soon as the norther had passed, he engaged Theodore Kremer as a cook at $20.00 per month, paid Vance and Brothers $142.50 for groceries and $16.50 for clothes, settled all his other outstanding accounts, engaged wagons to haul his supplies and equipment, and at nine o'clock on the morning of April 7, commenced his journey to Camp Cooper with thirty horses for the regiment, two wagons and twenty-five men, traveling via Fort Mason.

Lee had found the servant problem difficult to solve, for it was hard to find anyone of experience willing to risk his scalp in the Indian country. While in Indianola he had written Mary that "My servants have informed me they cannot go back to Camp Cooper. It is too dreary." In San Antonio he was pleased, therefore, to have Kremer accept employment. He was dubious whether or not he could cook and promised to give him a trial "out on the prairie."

At times Lee did not travel the regular road from Fort Mason to Camp Cooper. He later explained to a friend that by staying away from the well-beaten paths, he could find better camping sites, better grass for his horses, and stood less chance of meeting hostile Indians. When night came, he was tired and seldom thought of danger, even though he might be in an unsettled region. The nights were quiet and the stars friendly. He could banish care and find rest and sleep.

Lee arrived at Camp Cooper on April 18, 1857— eight months and sixteen days since he had left it for the court-martial at Ringgold Barracks. He had traveled almost two thousand miles since leaving his post. "Resumed my old tent," he entered in his "Memo. Book." "Found it very delapidated and things scattered."

At his "Texas home," however, still another court-martial awaited him. Lieutenant Robert N. Eagle was charged with a minor infraction of duty, which Lee thought was trivial, although he was to serve as president of the court; and on May 5 this trial, too, was adjourned sine die.

VI

"A Desert of Dullness"

L EE found his effects at Camp Cooper in better condition than he had expected, although his tent had been flattened by the wind several times and his dishes broken. Most of his livestock had disappeared, but otherwise his property was all there. Probably the Comanches had stolen his animals, for on the journey home he had heard rumors of their raids. He was so inured to danger on the border, however, that he did not fear them. At night he had felt as secure as in a crowded city and had brought his convoy through safely, with only five men to guard thirty horses. "I know in whose powerful hands I am," he explained, "and on them rely, and feel that in all life we are upheld and sustained by Divine Providence."

Just after Lee's return from Fort Brown an April norther zoomed down the valley of the Clear Fork, as intensely cold as any of winter; and Lee found the camp just as lonely a station as when he had left it for the Rio Grande. Katumse and his people were still trying to farm, without much success. "I wish there was anything interesting here to relate to you," he wrote Mary shortly after he arrived, "but we are in a desert of dullness, out of which nothing is drawn." Again a drought was threatening, repeating the pattern of the previous spring. Eight days after Lee had reached Camp Cooper, while the temperature stood at eighty-nine degrees, he was sitting in his shirt sleeves during the fore part of the night engaged in writing, when a second norther came roaring down, requiring heavier clothes and blankets before morning.

At least for a short period during this "desert of dullness" Lieutenant Eagle's court-martial furnished Lee temporary interest. He enjoyed the visit of Colonel Bainbridge; and Majors Thomas, Van Dorn, Paul, Captain King, and other officers were on the jury.

Major Thomas was accompanied to Camp Cooper by Mrs. Thomas; and Lee, a careful host, was driven to distraction. His "man, Kremer," was both awkward and unskilled in preparing food other than bread and beef, and the commissary could furnish no variety. Lee could depend on its preserved vegetables and fruits, but he thought this hardly enough for his guests when he remembered the elaborate table Mrs. Thomas had recently spread for him at San Antonio. How could he offer her just the rough fare of the border? He knew that Major Thomas would expect only what border officers customarily ate, but Mrs. Thomas should have better fare. In his plight he sent Kremer down the river to the nearest ranch to procure butter, milk, and poultry; and the servant presently came back to the post with "a few eggs, some butter and one old hen." Lee decided that he would not serve the "old hen" to dainty Mrs. Thomas, even though, he said, "game is few now and out of season and we are getting none of it." Greatly concerned, he wrote Mrs. Lee that he would inform her later how he "got on" with entertaining, but he overlooked reporting the results in other letters.

As May wore on, dust filled the air. On May 18 Lee wrote: "I must stop and look to my tent for there is a dust storm raging that sifts through everything and clogs my pen while I write. The thermometer is ninety-nine on the north side of my tent in a stiff breeze." Indeed, the "stiff breeze" brought no relief. A short time later, in the afternoon, the temperature stood at the 105-degree mark, although the wind was blowing steadily. The trees sighed mournfully and vegetation sickened. Once more drought visited the Clear Fork country. Day after day heat made Camp Cooper's tents and jacales insufferably hot. Dull red skies greeted the morning, afternoon clouds seemed thin and waterless, and promising early gardens turned brown, then shriveled and died, much to the discouragement of the soldiers.

So again dysentery, scurvy, fever, and other summer afflictions sent many patients to Dr. Gaenslen's two hospital tents, where heat from the canvas tops only added to their misery. And death struck again. A bright little boy, an only child, died, and his parents were prostrated with grief. They asked Lee to officiate at the funeral since there was no minister present. "So for the first time," he wrote Mary, " I read the beautiful funeral service of our church over the grave to a large and attentive audience of soldiers. The family were much affected." His men must have wondered what manner of man could reach such heights of military fame during the Mexican War as to be cited again and again for bravery and fearlessness and later as a sympathetic friend minister to the spiritual needs of grief-stricken parents.

July was equally trying. The drought increased in destructiveness, and the thermometer ranged above one hundred degrees, although sickness was on the decrease. But death claimed its second victim, another little boy, the son of one of Lee's sergeants. Lee had admired the child only the day before his illness, much to the pride of his parents. Then the dreadful malady struck quickly and fatally. The sergeant came to Lee, as he had on other matters, tears flowing down his cheeks, and asked him to read the funeral service as he had for the other victim. For the second time Lee performed this sad rite. It was his duty, he felt, although his spirit quailed within him. "I hope I shall not be called on again," he wrote Mary, "for though I believe that it is far better for the child to be called by his heavenly Creator into his presence in its purity and innocence, unpolluted by sin and uncontaminated by the vices of the world, still it so wrings a parent's heart with anguish that it is painful to see. Yet I know it was done in mercy to both—mercy to the child, mercy to the parents. The former has been saved from sin and misery here, and the latter have been given a touching appeal and powerful inducement to prepare for the hereafter."

Long rides up and down the Clear Fork or across the rolling hills in search of a new location for Camp Cooper helped Lee to forget his sadness. As early as December 5, 1856, Colonel Albert Sidney Johnston had written to Adjutant General Samuel Cooper that the site of Camp Cooper would probably be changed in the spring to some other place on the reserve or near by and that Lee would locate it after his return from Fort Brown. On March 10 he had instructed Lee to seek a suitable place. If he found a site only outside the Indian reservation, he was to negotiate a lease from the owner and to prepare plans for the buildings.

Daily Lee rode out from the post, sometimes alone but more often accompanied by one or more of his junior officers. The meandering river, its fine pecan, elm, and hackberry forests, an occasional ranch, and the unspoiled frontier wilderness always interested him. Riding along the quiet river, across the post-oak flats, ravines, and creeks brought him the freshness and vigor of border life, as well as the friendly, intimate companionship of admiring junior officers. As they rode along these trackless wilds, the younger officers confided in him as they might in their fathers, and Lee accepted with gentle understanding this unconscious tribute. In later years General Joseph E. Johnston, who had been closely associated with Lee during the Mexican War, explained: "He [Lee] was the only one of all the men I have known who could laugh at the faults and follies of his friends in such a manner as to make them ashamed without touching their affection for him, and to confirm their respect and sense of his superiority." Lee accounted for his own reserve in a letter to Fitzhugh: "I hope you will make many friends," he said, " . . . but indiscriminate intimacies you will find annoying and entangling, and they can be avoided by politeness and civility."

Lieutenant John B. Hood, one of Lee's West Point cadets who later became a prominent Southern commander, in his *Advance and Retreat,* told of an intimate conversation with Lee on one occasion. "Whilst riding with him upon one of these excursions, and enjoying the scenery and balmy air as we passed over the high undulating prairies of that beautiful region, the conversation turned upon matrimony, when he said to me with all the earnestness of a parent: 'Never marry unless you can do so into a family which will enable your children to feel proud of both sides of the house.' He perhaps thought I might form an attachment for some of the country lasses and therefore imparted to me his correct, and at the same time, aristocratic views in regard to this very important step in life. His uniform kindness to me whilst I was a cadet, inclined me the more willingly to receive and remember this fatherly advice; and from these early relations first sprang my affection and veneration which grew in strength to the end of his eventful career."

Lee had the happy faculty of retaining friends and of having their friendship grow into near devotion. Even General Scott was no exception. While Lee was making new, devoted friends on the border, Scott was using his influence to secure a lieutenant's commission for Lee's son Fitzhugh. "I make this application mainly on the extraordinary merits of the father," Scott wrote Secretary of War John B. Floyd, "the very best soldier that I ever saw in the field." Then he added that the son, too, was a remarkable youth, about twenty years of age, of fine stature and in fine health, a good linguist, a good mathematician, and about to graduate at Harvard. "He is also honorable and amiable like his father," he added, "and dying to enter the army." The commission was promptly granted.

Lee's interests on these rides were not always spiritual and philosophical. For instance, his love for cats manifested itself again. A cat would make his tent more homelike; and on his rides out from the post, he inquired at ranches for a cat, a cat that was yellow with spots on its back. Finally he learned of a litter of kittens at a ranch down the river, one of which the cowman promised him as soon as it was old enough to take away from its mother. Lee lightly admonished the donor that his cat must have at least one yellow spot on its coat.

Monotony was occasionally broken by an Indian scare. One morning during the latter part of June two Comanche scouts rode into camp bringing the news that a body of Indians was coming down from the north to attack the reserve. The scouts said that two of the hostile warriors had approached them about twenty miles north of Camp Cooper to entice them into their camp, but that instead they had returned as quickly as they could to bring the alarming news. These tidings threw Katumse's camp into great excitement, and the warriors kept their horses saddled all night. But morning found them undisturbed. "I confess I was incredulous and went to bed with no expectation of being aroused," Lee wrote. "I believe their apprehensions have somewhat subsided."

However, the search for a new site for the post went on, and even the enlisted men became deeply interested in it, for the weather remained warm and the Camp Cooper valley was like a bake oven. Lee also sought new springs that would relieve the camp's water shortage, because the supply at the post was failing, the river water was not drinkable during summer, and Camp Cooper's well was "gyp." On one of his rides Lee found a seepage in a ravine and immediately dispatched a fatigue party to dig springs. Meanwhile, on June 29, the thermometer registered 112 degrees, an additional incentive to find a cooler location for the post.

Although Lee spent much time in looking for a new

post site, he had improved Camp Cooper as best he could with materials at hand. For more than twelve months, fatigue parties of enlisted men had been sent into the post-oak woods north of the Clear Fork and to a near-by quarry for logs, clapboards, pickets, and building stone; while still others built thirteen structures about the parade ground, in the shape of a large "L." Captain Caldwell's quarters, the bakehouse, three company kitchens, and the guardhouse were made of stone with clapboard or canvas roofs; and the forage and quartermaster storehouses and two stables for the Second Cavalry horses were of logs. Other structures were of a more temporary character. Lee's quarters, as well as those of the other commissioned officers and enlisted men, and the two hospital structures were jacal with part-canvas sides and roof.

Lieutenant Herman Biggs of the First Infantry had made a full report on these improvements to Major D. H. Vinton, quartermaster, on May 24, 1857. He had also mentioned those factors which would materially relate to the building and maintenance of a permanent post. *"Building Material,* limestone in the immediate vicinity in abundance. . . . *Water*—sufficient thus far, of medium quality, procured by post wagons. . . . *Fuel*—quantity limited, mesquite, quality, ordinary, cost nothing, procured by company wagons, facilities for procuring, very bad. . . . *Forage*—quantity small, quality good, cost (of corn) $2.09 per bushel, obtained on contract. . . . *Beef*—quantity sufficient, quality good, cost 5¼ cents per pound, obtained on contract. . . . *Hay*—quantity limited, quality good, cost $20 per ton, obtained on contract, few facilities for procuring it. . . . *Roads*—condition, now good; distance to Ft. Belknap, 40 miles cross the Clear Fork of the Brazos; to Ft. Chadbourne, 100 miles, cross the Clear Fork of the Brazos and tributaries; to Camp Colorado, 110 miles, cross the Clear Fork and small tributaries of it; to Ft. Mason, 165 miles; to San Antonio, 275 miles. All the above rivers and streams are forded. Water is found on the road at convenient distances. *Transportation*—by government trains. And *Supplies*—except those already named received from San Antonio by Government trains, quality good."

So much sickness and death at Camp Cooper reminded Lee of his wife's failing health, but he was relieved when she wrote him that she would return to Berkeley Springs, Virginia, for the benefit of the hot baths; and that his brother-in-law, Mr. Childe, would accompany her. "See how kind our Heavenly Father is to us," he wrote her on July 5. "He always arranges for us better than we could do for ourselves."

The preceding day had been the second Fourth of July Lee had spent in Texas, and again his mind reverted to happy domestic scenes at Arlington on other holidays. This second Fourth, however, was not so lonely as that spent on his Comanche reconnaissance. His duties were so many and varied that he now had little time for repining. He also found interest in looking after the social and religious welfare of his men. Only a few days prior to the Fourth, Father Shane and Captain John M. Jones of Fort Belknap had visited Camp Cooper, and in a company kitchen a religious service was held, attended by only a small number of men. Lee could not understand the Latin part of the service, but he liked the priest's sermon on the text: "What will it profit a man if he gains the whole world and loses his own soul." He wrote later that he hoped the priest's words would sink deep into the hearts of the attentive soldiers.

On July 16, 1857, Lee received Special Order No. 89, assigning him to still another court-martial, this time at Fort Mason. Six days later he left Camp Cooper for the last time, turning over the command of the post to Captain Caldwell. Hardly had the trial started when he received a message ordering him to take command of the Second Cavalry at San Antonio, in place of Colonel Johnston who was being ordered to Washington. Promptly Lee and Johnston boarded the stage for San Antonio.

Fredericksburg was a favorite stopping place for travelers to San Antonio. It was a clean, progressive town settled by the German immigrants of a decade past. Lee always found the food at the town hotel tasty and varied and the accommodations as good as could be found in San Antonio. At night he was furnished a neatly kept room with oak furniture, a clean bed, and a homespun carpet. The room had two large curtained windows with roses trained above them on the outside, a sofa, a tall bureau upon which were a few books and a porcelain statuette, potted plants, a brass study lamp, a large ewer and wash basin, and towels.

Lee thoroughly enjoyed talking with the Fredericksburg residents about their migrations, their experiences on the border, and their plans and prospects; but his military duties never permitted him a lengthy stay.

San Antonio was also a town of never-ending interest, although Lee gave few details about it in his letters home. Fortunately, however, Frederick Law Olmsted, an Eastern traveler, visited it about the same time that Lee came to take command of the Second Cavalry, and in his *A*

Journey Through Texas, described it well. He was impressed with its singular heterogeneity, a change that had come since Lee had visited it first in 1846. Upon entering the town from the north, he noticed the outlying German homes of fresh square-cut blocks of creamy-white limestone, mostly of a single story and humble proportions but neat and thoroughly roofed and finished. Some houses had small bow windows, balconies, or galleries.

He entered Commerce Street by way of a bridge over the San Antonio River. This was the narrow, principal thoroughfare, where he saw American houses, and the breaking out of "the triple nationalities into an amazing display," till he reached the main plaza. About the pavement of the plaza the sauntering Mexicans prevailed, but bearded Germans and sallow Yankees furnished variety. "The signs," he said, "are by all odds German, and perhaps the houses, trim-built, with pink window-blinds."

The American dwellings stood back, with galleries and jalousies and garden picket fences against the walk, or rose in three-story brick to respectable city fronts. The Mexican buildings were stronger than he had seen elsewhere and were used for several purposes. They were all low, of stone or adobe, washed blue and yellow, with flat roofs close down upon their single story. "Windows had been knocked in their blank walls, letting the sun into their gloomy vaults," and most of them were stored with dry goods and groceries, which overflowed around the doors. At intervals about the plaza were American hotels and new glass-front stores, alternating with sturdy, battlemented Spanish walls and confronted by the dirty, grim, old, stuccoed stone cathedral, whose cracked bell, in discordant tones, called its worshipers to vespers, as though to repel the intruding race who had brought progress, while the cathedral dome frowned down from its imperturbable height. This was the San Antonio to which Lee came, to mingle with its even-flowing life and its tranquil indifference to change.

Lee and Johnston arrived in San Antonio on July 27, and Lee secured board at Mrs. Philips' Hotel facing the plaza. But he made arrangements with Johnston to occupy his home while he was away. Then he found time to write Mrs. Lee, explaining: "General Twiggs commander of the department has directed me to take up my abode here, which I shall therefore have to do; but, except so far as it puts me in quicker communication with you, the change to me is not desirable. I prefer the wilderness of Texas to its cities. In a few days, however, when the matter is fixed, I will rent me a little house on the bank of the San Antonio where I can at least enjoy bathing." A careful study of Lee's letters to members of his family shortly after his arrival in Texas and those of this period indicate that there had been a definite change in his point of view. Earlier he had evinced little interest in border life and problems; but now he could deliberately prefer a remote station and enjoy its solitude.

At San Antonio Johnston learned that he was to lead an expedition against the Mormons of Utah, who had refused to accept the jurisdiction of federal courts and were generally suspicious and resentful of all federal officials, civil and military. Lee feared that General Scott would withdraw the Second Cavalry from the Texas border for service with Johnston, but he was relieved to learn that this was not contemplated.

Shortly after he had arrived in San Antonio, Lee learned that his son "Rooney" (Fitzhugh) had received his commission as a second lieutenant and was on his way to California to join his officer brother, Custis. He was pleased and wrote Mary that this would start their sons on military careers, but that it pained him to realize that it would probably bring separation from their family.

On October 21 Mrs. Lee wired her husband that her father, George Washington Parke Custis, had passed away. Lee was shocked. The news was "as unexpected as afflicting," he wrote in his "Memo. Book." He was gravely concerned, for he knew that his sick wife was unable to solve the many problems arising as a result of her father's death. Immediately he made plans to go to her, relinquishing command of the Second Cavalry to Thomas and transferring the regiment's headquarters back to Fort Mason. Two days later he sold his mare and equipment to Lieutenant Grahame, paid his "little bills," gave Kremer his wages, took leave of his friends, and left San Antonio for a long stay in Virginia before he would again see Texas.

VII

"That Myth Cortinas"

WHEN Lee returned to Arlington, late fall had settled on the Virginia hills along the Potomac, bringing beauty and color to trees and shrubs. But he found Arlington itself in a sad state of neglect and disrepair. His father-in-law during his declining months had sought to put on canvas the scenes of Washington's battles before they faded from his memory; and the Arlington slaves had taken advantage of his preoccupation and failing interest to shirk plantation duties, tending only their own gardens and fishing in the Potomac. As a consequence, bushes and weeds had invaded the spacious lawn, roofs of the mansion and barns had begun to leak, and fields had gone untilled.

For several reasons this home-coming was not as happy for Lee as others had been. In addition to the grief occasioned by Mr. Custis's death, he found Mrs. Lee threatened by complete invalidism from arthritis, an affliction she had carefully kept from her soldier husband while he was in Texas. Also, he felt keenly the absence of his two sons who were attached to military organizations in the West, and he was further grieved by the illness of two of his daughters. In deep sorrow he wrote to Custis in California that there was little left in life for him. Under compelling duty, however, he soon threw off his "somber

phiz," sent Mrs. Lee away to the Hot Springs for the benefit of the baths, and sought to solve the most pressing of
his new domestic problems.

He was primarily concerned at this time with his
father-in-law's will. The old gentleman had divided his
estate among Lee's family. His three plantations of Arlington, the "White House," and Romancock were left to
his three grandsons, Custis, "Rooney," and Rob, respec-
tively, although Mrs. Lee was to be mistress of Arlington
until her death. To each of his granddaughters, he left
$10,000, to be provided by the sale of Smith's Island, off
Northampton County, and lands in Stafford, Richmond,
and Westmoreland counties, augmented if necessary from
the income from the "White House" and Romancock.
This provision was doubly difficult to meet since the
plantations had a heavy indebtedness against them. Like-
wise, it brought complication in probating the will and
caused long delay in the Virginia court, necessitating ex-
tensions of Lee's absence from his regiment until February 6, 1860. Lee was sole executor of the will, a role
that was difficult but not altogether unpleasant, for every
member of his family was considerate and understanding.
He himself received from the estate only a lot in "Square
21" of Washington City. The will also provided for free-
ing the slaves of the plantations "in not exceeding five
years" from his father-in-law's demise.

By midsummer of 1858 conditions at Arlington had
improved. Under Lee's strict supervision, the slaves had
laid aside their fishing poles for plows and hoes, and the
fields had been planted to corn and other crops. Hedges
were trimmed, houses repaired, and fences rebuilt. Lee's
days were filled with arduous and varied tasks. He visited

his old friend, General Scott, to secure a Washington appointment for Custis, so that he would be near Arlington, of which later he would be proprietor; he sought the advice of Alexandria lawyers regarding the will; and he pushed ahead with improvements to the plantation.

While Lee was thus engaged, on October 17, 1859, Lieutenant "Jeb" Stuart brought him an order from Colonel Drinkard to report immediately to the Secretary of War for duty; and Lee complied so promptly that he did not take time to change from civilian garb to military uniform. He and Stuart crossed the Potomac immediately and reported to Secretary John B. Floyd, who assigned Lee to quell the John Brown disturbance at Harpers Ferry.

John Brown and nineteen followers had raided Harpers Ferry on the night of October 16, when they had seized the Baltimore and Ohio Railroad bridge crossing from the Maryland side of the Potomac to Harpers Ferry in Virginia. The fanatical band had cut the telegraph wires, occupied the United States arsenal, and begun a campaign to free the slaves by visiting Colonel Lewis Washington's plantation in the dead of night, arresting its owner, and inviting his slaves to join them in their liberation move. The next morning (October 17) the citizens of Harpers Ferry seized the raiders' weapons, cut them off from retreat to Maryland; and forced them to barricade themselves, together with several hostages whom they had captured, in the enginehouse of the armory yard.

Floyd was not in possession of all these facts when he sent for Lee. He had only heard that a band of desperate men had seized the arsenal. Before he gave Lee his in-

Brownsville, Texas, about 1857

From a contemporary engraving

structions, therefore, he and Lee called on President James Buchanan, who with "several members of his Cabinet were endeavoring to learn the cause and extent of the trouble from telegraphic dispatches from Baltimore." But when they could furnish no additional news, Floyd instructed Lee to take command of a detachment of marines and to proceed at once to the scene of disturbance to restore peace and order and to arrest the offenders. Other troops would be sent on later.

Lee executed his order promptly. Stuart accompanied him to Harpers Ferry and acted as his messenger by visiting the arsenal under a white flag to demand the surrender of Brown and his confederates. When Brown refused to comply unless he and his men would be allowed to recross the Potomac to the Maryland side, Lee ordered Lieutenant Green and a squad of twelve marines to batter down the door of the enginehouse and arrest the defenders. In his "Memo. Book" Lee thus explained what followed: "About sunrise with twelve marines under the command of Lieutenant Green, . . . broke in the door of the engine house, secured the robbers and released the prisoners unhurt. All [robbers] were killed or mortally wounded but four—John Brown, Aaron Stevens, Edwin Coffee and Guin Shields (black). He had the prisoners moved to a place of safety and their wounds dressed." Later Brown was tried in a Virginia court, found guilty of treason, and hanged on December 2, manifesting the utmost composure until the end. Lee seemed not to sense the significance of Brown's action but viewed him only as an unbalanced fanatic who had led a band of ignorant men into open outlawry.

Back at Arlington on February 6, 1860, Lee at last

received an order to return to Texas to assume temporary command of the department, with headquarters at San Antonio. One cannot doubt that his leaving was under happier circumstances than his coming to Arlington. Mary's health was improved, Custis had received his Washington assignment, and the interests of other members of his family had been properly safeguarded. At last he could resume his service as a border soldier. Still he found it hard to leave his afflicted wife, explaining to her, "My departures grow harder to bear with years."

At New Orleans, while en route to Texas, Lee wrote Custis that he had left home so hurriedly that he had forgotten some of his personal belongings. "Imagine my horror this morning," he said, "when I found I had left my shaving-brush and pants behind. The first I constantly leave, but my pants, my *new pants,* I cannot account for. . . . I could hardly believe my own eyes when I found them out of their accustomed place. Take care of them, or use them as may be most convenient."

He arrived at Indianola at twelve o'clock noon on February 19 and at San Antonio two days later. He found lodging with his old landlady, Mrs. Philips, in the plaza, since he did not know how long he would remain in San Antonio. On the following day he formally took command, succeeding Colonel Washington Seawell.

Lee's former acquaintances welcomed him back to San Antonio. "They wonder why I do not have you all out," he wrote his daughter Annie. "They do not know your capacity." Once again he took up his pleasant custom of visiting in the homes of his fellow officers and enjoying their hospitality.

There were also social affairs given by civilians. Mrs.

Kate Merrett Clarkson told of a gathering at Dr. McCormick's home, when the Doctor's stepdaughter, Nannie, had invited her to help entertain. "The guests included Colonel Robert E. Lee," she said. "Some of the girls were asked to play the piano, but in their timidity made many excuses. Colonel Lee then asked me to play, and though I was the youngest girl there, my mother had always taught me never to refuse to do my best, so I made my bow and played for the company. Colonel Lee, who had led me to the piano and stood by my side, thanked me in most gracious terms and when supper was announced he took me in to supper. . . . I shall never forget Colonel Lee as one of the most charming and gracious gentlemen I ever met."

Lee was pleased and flattered by this attention, but it did not distract him from the duties at hand. Busy days were ahead of him. New posts must be established, his cavalry units reassigned, and a multitude of minor matters attended to. All these tasks left him little time to scan the political horizon. Had he done so, the angry mutterings of sectionalists, North and South, would have given him grave concern.

Lee's duties as department commander taxed his patience and ability. Routine matters such as troop changes, buying sites for military posts, and reviewing discipline cases took up much of his time; but he gave each subject his personal attention. In every way he sought to humanize the service. Military penalties were ordinarily harsh. Absence without leave, drunken brawls, and even minor infractions of regulations drew heavy punishment, such as branding with a hot iron, flogging, or carrying a thirty-

or forty-pound rock or log all day every day for a month. Whenever these rigorous disciplines were called to his attention, he either modified or disapproved them, and his attitude caused the enlisted men to regard him as their protector.

Governor Sam Houston of Texas complained to Lee of border turmoil because of Indian and Mexican raids. He had also appealed earlier for aid to President Buchanan and to Secretary of War John B. Floyd. In reply Floyd, as all good secretaries should, assured him that everything possible was being done for the distressed frontier, even to the point of sending Lee as new department commander, "an officer of great discretion and ability." Now Houston learned that Lee was worthy of Floyd's praise. He worked with energy to bring immediate relief to the exposed frontier, and he represented with dignity every interest of the Department of Texas and the federal government.

Most of his first office chores were done under the handicap of a common cold. The evening of March 1 had been still and warm, but during the night a norther blew up, sending the mercury tumbling and causing Lee's physical distress. Still he wrote Mrs. Lee optimistically that the trees showed green and that spring was on its way to San Antonio.

Most annoying of all nuisances was the effort of a promoter, P. L. Lea, to enlist his aid in a filibustering expedition against Mexico. He had met Lea at Indianola on his journey back to Texas, and the promoter had become his traveling companion as far as Victoria. Lee had rebuffed his advances, stating diplomatically that he could serve only the interests of the United States, and as an army officer. Lea informed his brother, A. M. Lea, of his failure to enlist the Virginian; and, in turn, A. M., who was equally interested in the proposed filibuster, transmitted this information to Sam Houston, who had, indeed, originated the plan.

Houston was a resourceful Jacksonian democrat with a checkered political career. He had served with Jackson during the Creek War of 1814 and had been elected governor of Tennessee in 1828, only to resign shortly after he came to office and leave his wife to go into Indian Territory to live among the Indians. Later he emerged from this self-imposed exile to take part in the Texas revolution, to win victory over Santa Anna at San Jacinto, to be twice elected president of the Texas republic, to serve three terms in the United States Senate, and finally to be elected governor of Texas, the office he held when Lee became department commander. Houston had seasoned this ripe and varied experience with political sagacity. He was essentially honest, forceful, far sighted, and patriotic; moreover, he had built up a political following of able men.

He had early conceived of a Mexican protectorate, and on February 16, 1858, he had made a proposal concerning one in a bill to the Senate, but it had been summarily rejected. He was not easily defeated, however, and continued to dream and plan. Available correspondence is insufficient to prove that the Leas approached Lee at Houston's suggestion, but it seems probable that they did. While Lee was en route to Texas, Houston, piqued, had written Secretary Floyd about troubles along the Rio Grande, saying: "But matters new and startling arise, and he [Houston] may feel that it is his duty to meet the emergency in carrying his action so far as to not only repel the aggressions from Mexico, but to adopt such measures as will prevent the recurrence of similar inroads upon our frontiers." He said that Texas could muster 10,000 troops for this purpose within thirty days, "to make reclamation upon Mexico for all her wrongs."

In reporting his brother's rebuff by Lee, A. M. Lea slyly suggested to Houston: "He [Lee] would not touch anything he would consider vulgar filibustering, but he is not without ambition, and *under the sanction of the Govt.* might be more willing to aid you to pacificate Mexico." And knowing that Houston was also a man of ambition, Lea cunningly added: "If the people of the United States should recall you from the 'Halls of the Montezumas' to the 'White House' at Washington, you would find him well fitted to carry out your great idea of a Protectorate. . . . You see that Providence is guiding you on to the consummation of your grand conception of the Protectorate almost in spite of yourself." In explaining why Lee was ideally cast for such a "Protectorate," Lea said that he was "well informed in matters of State, honest, modest, brave and skillful."

Lea approached Lee more than once, setting forth the vast advantages of the Mexican venture. But Lee refused with his usual courtesy and restraint. He wrote Lea on March 1 that he had recently received three letters from him, all in the same mail, and added, "I feel that I owe to your kindness rather than to my merit, your recommendations to Governor Houston." He said that he had first become acquainted with Houston while he was a cadet at West Point. Houston had been president of the board of visitors one year and had made an impression on him that had not been effaced during the many years since. "I have followed with interest his career," he continued, "and have admired his manly qualities and conservative principles. His last position in favour of the Constitution and Union elicits my cordial approbation."

But he was still firm in his refusal to take a part in filibustering. "Should military force be required to quiet our Mexican frontier," he said, "I have no doubt that arrangements will be made to maintain the rights and peace of Texas, and, I hope, in conformity to the Constitution and laws of the country. It will give me great pleasure to do all in my power to support both." Nor would he go to Aransas Bay to appraise its port facilities, at Lea's suggestion; he was sufficiently aware of its advantages without a personal inspection. In closing, he promised that Lea could rely upon his "not mentioning the plans, preparations or views of the Comps. [railroad promoters] until disclosed by themselves."

Lea evidently regarded this as a dismissal, but he did not abandon his plan. He forwarded Lee's letter to Houston under a note marked "Private," ingratiatingly suggesting: "Although it is plain from his [Lee's] allusion to the 'Constitution and the laws' that he would not participate in any movement upon Mexico not expressly sanctioned by the Government, yet his expressions towards yourself are so justly complimentary that I thought that you would be glad to see them, coming as they do from a man of high intelligence and sincerity. You see, indeed, that they were designed for no eye but mine." Then reverting to his more immediate interest, he complained: "So Mr. Buchanan violated his repeated promise to have the rights of the Rio G. Mex. and Pac. R. R. Co.

guaranteed in the Mexican Treaty and got his treaty defeated thereby in the Senate. I send you a map showing the proposed 'central transit,' and a copy of my brother's memorial to the Senate.''

No doubt Houston was disappointed. A Mexican protectorate had become a fixed ambition. Perhaps he had dreamed of the day when he would be elected President of the United States on the strength of it. Then he could send Lee, the eminent military genius, to take control of his newly won domain south of the Rio Grande. But Lee would not approve his plan. Houston was too old, and civil war clouds loomed too ominously for him to recast it. Throughout all his planning, he seemed to have no thought of Mexican oppression. He believed that the Mexican people would welcome an end to their exploitation by military cliques and that a firm, progressive government would bring prosperity to the country.

Cortinas's antics along the Rio Grande caused Lee to forget the filibustering proposal. Juan Nepomuceno Cortinas had long caused trouble. He was a *ranchero*, at one time claiming to be an American and at another a Mexican citizen. Walter Prescott Webb says that he "was the black sheep of his mother's otherwise commendable flock. Though his brothers and sisters were cultured and educated, Juan was impervious to all good influences. He successfully resisted education, did not learn to read, and only learned to sign his name after he became governor of Tamaulipas.''[1] When Lee had been with Wool on the Rio Grande, Cortinas had been a soldier in General Arista's army. And in the years since then he had been

[1] *The Texas Rangers, a Century of Frontier Defense* (Houghton Mifflin Company, Boston, New York, 1935), 176.

noted as a lawless, desperate man. In 1850 he had been indicted at Brownsville for murder, and the sheriff's attempt to arrest him caused him to hide out until the witnesses were gone. After four years he had again appeared, but no effort had been made to arrest him until 1859, when he was charged with horse stealing. Once more he became a Jean Valjean, a fugitive from justice, whose Javert, repeatedly seeking his arrest, was Adolphus Glavaecke. Knowing that he was a marked man, when he showed up on Brownsville's streets, he was accompanied by his henchmen, who made it dangerous for an officer of the law to attempt his arrest. His principal business was dealing in stock, purchasing or stealing, as was most convenient. He was a great hero among the Mexican *peones,* and, since he controlled many votes, he was courted by politicians at election time.

A few miles out of Brownsville was his rancho, San José, to which he would retire when officers sought to arrest him. Here he would surround himself with desperate outlaws and could very well defy peace officers. On July 13, 1859, he went to Brownsville with some of his gang. The city marshal, Robert Shears, arrested one of them for abusing a coffeehouse keeper. Cortinas interfered and fired twice at the marshal, the second shot wounding him in the shoulder. He then quickly mounted his horse, took the prisoner up behind him, and rode away with his men, defying the authorities to arrest him. In Matamoros he was treated as a hero and defender of Mexican rights.

This defiance of authority aroused Brownsville. The sheriff organized a posse to go after Cortinas, but when he learned that Cortinas had a stronger force, he disbanded his men. The news of this action was quickly relayed to the outlaw by sympathetic friends, and other Mexicans enlisted in his cause.

Major S. P. Heintzelman of the First Infantry, while at Brownsville a short time later, reported to Lee that Cortinas had held a captain's commission in the Mexican Army. He had been a lieutenant under General Guadalupe García, but had been detected selling government horses and had been dismissed. Later, with fifty men, he had sought to re-enlist, but García declined his offer.

Heintzelman also wrote Lee that Cortinas probably held a commission in the customhouse or maritime guards, and using it as a pretext, had recruited men and purchased arms. The bandit's first cousin, Don Miguel Tijerina, on September 28, had told friends in Brownsville that Cortinas "was a desperate, contrary fellow. When every one thought that he had started for the interior he turned up suddenly in Brownsville." Heintzelman heard that he had returned to kill all his enemies that he could catch, and then go into hiding.

This was just about what had happened. Before daylight, on September 28, 1859, Cortinas had entered Brownsville with a body of mounted men, estimated at from forty to eighty, leaving two small parties of footmen near the outskirts of town. The Brownsville residents had been awakened by the firing of guns and cries of *"Viva Cheno Cortinas!" "Mueran los gringos!" "Viva Mexico!"* Soon Cortinas held the city, with sentinels at the street corners and armed men riding about. He loudly threatened to kill all Americans but assured Mexicans and foreigners that they would not be harmed.

Lee was told that Cortinas had taken over Fort Brown, which had only recently been abandoned by United

States troops. A part of his men had sought to break in the door of the powder magazine without success, while others rode through the streets hunting their enemies. Some of them had stormed the jail, freed its prisoners, knocked off their shackles, and invited them to join the raid. In doing so, they had killed Jailer Johnson (who killed one of his assailants before he fell), Constable George Morris, a young man named Neale, and a Mexican; but they were more intent on seeking Glavaecke and Shears.

During the fighting, Cortinas had ridden up to a store near the river front and asked for spirits of turpentine. He had been seen by watchers from across the river. A few minutes later, General Caravajál had come to the levee with the expressed intention of stopping "all this"; and, seeing Tijerina, who commanded the Mexican cavalry, he had ordered him to cross over to his side of the river instantly. This he had done, on horseback, accompanied by Agopita Longoría. Caravajál then had sent for Cortinas and after a talk persuaded him to withdraw his men, numbering about fifty, to his mother's Santa Rita Rancho, about six miles west of town.

Meanwhile Anglo-Americans had sent out frantic appeals for help, both to state and federal officials. One of these, Collector of Customs Francis W. Larharn, of the District of Brazos de Santiago, had written an urgent letter to General D. E. Twiggs, while he was commander of the Department of Texas. "Last night a crowd of banditti of men, numbering fifty, entered this town, and committed the most inhuman and cold-blooded murders on the persons of three American citizens and one of Mexican origin," he began. He said that early the following morning Brownsville had asked for Mexican troops from Matamoros to protect them and that they had marched up to the river bank, ready to answer any emergency call. In fact, they later crossed the river and helped to protect the terror-stricken Anglo-Americans, who seemingly saw no irregularity in Mexican troops' protecting Americans against Mexicans on American soil! "Finally," said Larharn, "a truce was made until night, when the aforesaid Mexican gentlemen, Don Macedonio Capistran, Don Agopita Longoría, and Don Miguel Tijerina, myself accompanying them, went to their camp, about eight miles above this town, and, after persuasion, induced the crowd to disperse."

Cortinas did not rob the town, as he might well have done. He seemed only intent on finding and killing his enemies. But some of his men who were less inhibited, seized whatever liquor they could find.

From the Santa Rita Rancho, two days later, Cortinas had issued a proclamation, bidding defiance to the law, assuming protection of downtrodden Mexicans, and accusing Anglo lawyers of despoiling them of their lands, a charge that had at least some foundation. This, of course, elevated him to a lofty perch in the eyes of hero-worshiping Mexicans; and there was a general belief among them that Cortinas would drive the hated, oppressive gringos north of the Nueces.

At the same time this was a challenge that the Texans could not afford to ignore. The sheriff, with a posse, started up the river to visit the rancho and to reconnoiter its vicinity. While moving forward, his party captured Tomás Cabrera, Cortinas's second in command. When Cortinas, who was in Matamoros, heard of this, he demanded that the Brownsville citizens release Cabrera immediately or he would "lay the town in ashes." But the town authorities informed the message-bearer that Cabrera was in custody of the sheriff and would be dealt with by Texas law.

A few hours later Captain W. G. Tobin and a company of Texas Rangers arrived in Brownsville. These state troopers were certainly not up to the standard of the average rangers and respected law and order but little better than the Mexican outlaws, for on the night following their coming, either Cabrera was hanged by them, or they did not try to prevent others from committing the outrage.

During the same night Cortinas recrossed the river and took up his old quarters at his mother's rancho, collecting men and arms to carry out his threats. A few hours later his men appeared on the outskirts of Brownsville but found its citizens so heavily armed that they soon withdrew. Under the lead of W. B. Thompson, the Brownsville Tigers had been formed and were joined by Mexican militia under Colonel Loranco of Matamoros —a total force of about sixty men. This joint "army," with two cannon, moved out toward the Santa Rita Rancho on the morning of October 22, 1859, but Cortinas's men sent them flying back to Brownsville and captured their artillery. The Anglos may have been braver men than the Mexicans. If so, they wished to conserve their strength, for they beat their Mexican allies back to town by several hundred yards!

Now in possession of two fieldpieces, Cortinas could prove his military prowess. He could not only parade his men but also his cannon before admiring followers. After this he robbed and plundered at will, stopped the mail riders between Brownsville and Point Isabel, captured and cut open the mailbags and had the letters read to him. "Once," Heintzelman wrote Lee, "he sent in the letters opened, with a note apologizing to the postmaster, 'as it was a matter of necessity for him to know what steps were taken against him.' By this means he knew more of what was going on outside of Brownsville than its citizens." He had known, for instance, when Tobin's rangers were expected to arrive in Brownsville and had set a trap for them, but they came to town by another road and were unmolested.

After the arrival of Tobin's rangers other recruits joined in Brownsville's defense, until a force of about 250 men had assembled. Then under Tobin's command they moved out a second time toward Cortinas's position a short distance above town but retreated just as quickly as their predecessors. These failures only made the raider's position stronger, and adventurous Mexicans continued to join him. Santos Cadena, with forty men from Agua Leguas, arrived a short time after Tobin's defeat. They stayed until they had loaded themselves with plunder and then recrossed the Rio Grande to Mexico. Other recruits were convicts who had broken jail at Victoria, Tamaulipas.

It was at this juncture that United States troops came to Brownsville to take a hand in the affair. Cortinas had reached the high tide of his success. On December 5, 1859, Major Heintzelman, with 117 men, occupied Fort Brown and nine days later left Brownsville with his men and 120 others, including Tobin's rangers, to go after Cortinas. He found the Mexicans entrenched at La Ebronal and drove them from the field, killing eight Mexicans and losing one ranger and two of his regulars wounded. Then Major John S. Ford, with fifty-three additional rangers, joined the hunt for Cortinas and defeated him in a second battle at Rio Grande City on December 26. The Austin *Gazette* of January 14, 1860, reported that Ford had led his men in a mad charge, shouting "You d—d sons of b—s, we have got you!" Evidently the Mexicans thought so, too, for they fled panic stricken. Later, Cortinas placed his men at La Bolsa Bend on the Rio Grande to capture the steamer, *Ranchero,* known to be laden with a cargo valued at $300,000. But his move was anticipated by Heintzelman's and Ford's troops, and he was again defeated after a desperate battle, in which he lost twenty-nine killed and forty wounded.

After this fight Cortinas became a will-o'-the-wisp. The wings of fright and rumor had him at one place one day and at another, distant point the next. By the time Lee returned to San Antonio, in February, 1860, the whole of the Rio Grande Valley was seething with excitement. Lee listened with patience to repeated rumors and calls for help and, when they increased in volume, decided to visit the disturbed area. He wrote Mrs. Lee, referring to the raider as "that myth Cortinas," but expressing a determination to bring his depredations to an end.

Lee employed two former soldiers to serve him on the journey. They were unskilled as servants but were the best that he could hire. "Their skill in cooking," he wrote, "consists in making coffee, boiling rice and beans and frying ham or any fresh meat you may procure—that is, all you caught in the field, and with that I am content."

Accompanied by one company of cavalry, on March

15 Lee started for the Rio Grande. On his second day out, he received word that Cortinas was near Eagle Pass. Quickly he changed his course to meet this new threat. On his way to the Rio Grande, he overtook or passed only Mexicans driving their oxen, and he saw on the plains "a few mustangs, rattlesnakes, deer, antelopes, and one turkey." He said that he did not find one running stream and that grass along the road was poor. This was much the same experience that he had had on his earlier trip to the Rio Grande, but he was soon to be faced with a problem far more difficult and complicated than any he had yet met in Texas.

VIII

"A Rough Diplomatist"

ON the way to Eagle Pass Lee had opportunity to consider the various aspects of his problem. He had learned that Cortinas and his five hundred or more pillagers had laid waste the Rio Grande Valley from Brownsville to Rio Grande City, a distance of 120 miles, and back to the Arroyo Colorado. Anglo-Americans had abandoned the country as though fleeing from a scourge. The outlaws had either taken their horses and cattle or caused them to be scattered in the chaparral thickets, or their owners had driven them into Mexico. It was reported that they sold a cow and calf for as little as one dollar. Rio Grande City was almost depopulated, and only one family was left in Edinburg. Business for 240 miles above Brownsville had been interrupted or suspended for five months, and fields lay fallow. Claims of citizens against the federal government had piled up to the staggering sum of $336,826. Many of the claims were exaggerated, but many more were valid. The valley was swept not only by Cortinas's bands but also by the Texans. The Mexicans burned the ranchos belonging to persons against whom they had a grudge; and the Texans, in retaliation, destroyed those that were left. In all these raids and counterraids 15 Americans and 80 loyal Mexicans had been killed, and others had been wounded, while Cortinas had lost 151 men killed and many more wounded.

During all this turmoil and excitement residents of Brownsville had appealed to President Buchanan, Governor Houston, and any other officials, national or state, whom they thought might help them. A Brownsville grand jury had laid the blame at Mexico's door, charging that three-fourths of Cortinas's raiders resided in Mexico; that a short time earlier fifty men, in one body, under a Monterrey officer, had joined the outlaws; and that still later thirty to sixty "jailbirds" had come from Victoria, the capital of Tamaulipas. All these were given regular military training, marched under the Mexican flag, and openly proclaimed their allegiance to Mexico.

Lee did not know how widespread were these raids. If they were as threatening as his informants reported them to be, then he must switch additional cavalry units to the danger points. Washington officials had been nonplused. Some had wondered if these reports were hatched to promote Houston's "protectorate" plans, but Secretary Floyd at least was convinced that they were not and had ordered that corrective measures be taken. He had instructed Lee to notify Mexican authorities to "break up and disperse" the raiders then plundering the Rio Grande Valley and, if necessary, to "cause this to be done by the force under his command." In this event drastic action, which might cause friction with Mexico, would be necessary, but Lee felt that the occasion warranted the taking of strong measures. He had written Secretary Floyd that he would leave for the Rio Grande immediately, taking with him Captain Brackett's company of the Second Cavalry then at Camp Verde.

Lee was not many hours out of San Antonio before he had proof of border chaos. At the Sabinal he heard that raiding Indians had stolen some horses only a few hours before his arrival and that a posse was organizing for pursuit, led by the Kennedy brothers and a Mr. Knox of San Antonio, who, while encamped on the plains east of the river, had lost two of his best horses to the Indians. On the road farther west a Mrs. Hall told him that she and her husband had saved their horses only by brandishing pistols before the determined Indians who were trying to drive them from the corral. This was disquieting news, and Lee might have joined in the pursuit but for his orders to go to the Rio Grande.

Still, he reasoned, his trip to Eagle Pass might be fruitless, for he was acting on a report from a government contractor, a Mr. Duclos, who had heard that Cortinas outlaws were approaching the town. Near Eagle Pass Lee met the stagecoach and inquired of the driver about conditions in town. The driver replied that all was quiet, that Cortinas had not arrived, but that he was reported nearing Laredo, farther down the river. A short time later, when Lee rode into Eagle Pass, he found that it was as quiet as the stage driver had reported, that Duclos's story was "all flam and clap trap." Therefore, he halted there only long enough to write some letters, one of which was to Adjutant General Samuel Cooper, reporting that "Everything in this section of the country is quiet, and the usual intercourse and commerce between Mexico and the United States is uninterrupted." Then Lieutenant Eagle's company of the Second Cavalry joined him for his ride down the river toward Laredo.

Lee's force was impressive as it moved along the road.

The smartly groomed troopers astride excellent, sleek horses, guidons fluttering, and accoutrements glistening under a Texas sun, with cumbrous supply wagons bringing up the rear—all tended to warn venturesome and lawless men that the rights of the federal government were not to be trifled with. While on the march Lee had followed a strict schedule—reveille at 4 A. M., the start of the day's march at 5:30 A. M., and a final halt at 2 P. M. to graze the horses until dark.

Long hours of riding through sweltering heat were exhausting, but Lee was accustomed to rough campaigning. The lure of the trail and venturing beyond human habitation fascinated him. An evening sunset, breaking through rain clouds; the soft twilight, with his men silhouetted against their campfires; the dusky dome of the sky, studded with millions of glittering stars at bedtime; the blue dawns; and the approaching storm cloud, with its flashes of lightning and rumbling thunder—all to him were God's manifestations of power. The laughter and pleasing banter of his men enlivened the tiring ride through desert wastes. At noon or at night he heartily enjoyed the food his cook set before him. Boiled ham, rice, eggs, tomatoes, and molasses and bread, with a slice of sponge cake for dessert, made up his fare for supper, after which he could enjoy talking with his men until bedtime. "Now if I had one of my daughters to keep house for me," he wrote Mrs. Lee after one supper, "I would be set up."

But there were trying days, too. While he was at Laredo, a cold norther blew up, whipping about his troopers' exposed plateau camp. Lee could have stayed in town and toasted his feet before a warm fire, but his thoughts, as usual, turned first to his men. He ordered them to break camp and resume their journey down the river until they could find firewood. He lingered in town until he could load his wagons with corn, a task which was not completed until 1 P. M. By that time the hard-driving rain had changed to sleet and snow, and the ground was covered with an icy coating.

With loaded wagons Lee rode out of Laredo, wrapping his greatcoat about him for protection against the piercing wind. But at five o'clock he stopped to allow his wagons to catch up with him. He also expected to overtake his troopers, but they had stayed nearer the river. After he had halted, he heard their bugle and concluded that they had made a comfortable camp. Then he dismounted, spread out his blankets, and sought their warmth in restless sleep. But he was up at dawn, a teamster having made contact with the troopers during the night. When Lee rode into their camp, he found that they had suffered terribly from exposure and that two of them had died. Some of them had bought whiskey at Laredo, and at least one of the two men who had died of exposure had drunk enough of the liquor to make him heedless of proper precautions against the weather.

The storm lifted as suddenly as it had descended, and Lee and his men resumed their journey, making a comfortable camp the next night well down the river. From here the trip to Ringgold Barracks was without disturbing incident, the men finding the broken terrain and broad, sweeping mesquite and chaparral flats quite monotonous.

Rio Grande City and near-by Ringgold Barracks were yet visited with rumor and excited gossip about Cortinas.

Reliable residents told Lee, however, that Cortinas had fled southward, "some say alone, others with a few followers," Lee explained. Heintzelman reported that Cortinas had left for the Burgos Mountains, three days' march from the river, and that he probably would not concentrate another force on the Rio Grande.

While at Ringgold Barracks, Lee wrote a stern letter to Governor Andres Treviño of Tamaulipas, a letter strictly in keeping with his orders. "I have been instructed by the Secretary of War of the United States," he wrote, "to notify the authorities of Mexico on the Rio Grande frontier that they must break up and disperse the bands of banditti which have been concerned in these depredations and have sought protection within Mexican territory, and further, that they will be held responsible for the faithful performance of this plain duty on their part." He closed by "requesting" that the Governor disperse any bands within his jurisdiction.

Here the colorful Texan, Major Ford of the Texas Rangers, rode into town to report to Lee that his men were encamped about forty miles below. Lee received him with all the consideration due a brother officer. Ford was greatly impressed with his host and later wrote: "His [Lee's] appearance was dignified, without hauteur, grand, without pride, and in keeping with the noble simplicity characterizing a true republican. He evinced an imperturbable self-possession, and a complete control of his passions. To approach him was to feel yourself in the presence of a man of superior intellect, possessing the capacity to accomplish great ends, and the gift of controlling and leading men."

From Ringgold Barracks Lee moved into the region

recently devastated. It yet carried the scars of war—doorless and roofless jacales, smut-blackened chimneys standing amid rubble that once was ranch homes, gates torn from their hinges, broken-down fences, and untilled fields and empty barns. "The occupants," he observed, "had generally taken refuge in Mexico."

Lee's arrival at Edinburg, opposite Reynosa, was most opportune, for there was little less than war existing between these two towns, one American, the other Mexican. On the morning before his arrival Mexican soldiers had fired into Major Ford's Texas Rangers from across the Rio Grande. The fire had been returned, and two Mexicans had been severely wounded.

Lee took immediate steps to quiet the troubled waters by sending across the river Captain Brackett, bearing a white flag and a peace message for the Reynosa authorities. He was instructed to inquire into the cause of the firing and to demand that some of the outlaws, who were known to be in town, be delivered to the Americans. Brackett found all of Reynosa's streets barricaded and loaded cannon planted in front of the House of Justice. The town was guarded by four companies of Mexican troops, and re-enforcements were hourly expected from Camargo and Matamoros.

The message which Brackett bore was similar to that Lee had sent to Governor Treviño, except that it was more pointed. It warned the Reynosans that further depredations on the American side of the Rio Grande "cannot longer exist, and must be put an end to."

The message was an agreeable surprise to Reynosan authorities. They had expected an attack, but now it was possible to avoid further trouble. Quickly President

Zepeda of the town council called that body together to frame a reply. Hurriedly the council dispatched Zepeda to Lee with the answer. They refuted his charge that Reynosa had harbored Cortinas's men and stated that they, too, had orders to arrest and imprison "factious Cortinas" and his "skulking vagabonds" whenever they came to town. They said that in the past Reynosa had been known as a haven of refuge for Anglo-Americans fleeing from these robber bands. But they had not found the Anglos so circumspect. Only three days before Lee's arrival, they charged, Major Ford and about seventy Texans had crossed the Rio Grande and had occupied the town. Zepeda had warned the Major that he was violating the rights of a friendly nation and had told him that neither Cortinas nor any of his henchmen were in town, whereupon he had withdrawn. But later the Texans had fired on the Mexican *garita* (sentry box), wounding a Mexican river guard and a boy working in a nearby field.

Lee queried Ford about the Reynosan incident and was told that the Mexican account of it was substantially correct. Ford had heard that the town was harboring Cortinas outlaws and that some of the townsmen had joined with them in raids on the American side of the river. He had crossed the river with his rangers to punish the outlaws and to impress the Reynosans with their responsibility in keeping peace. But, he said, he had withdrawn from Mexico when the town leaders had assured him that the outlaws were not there.

Lee listened quietly to Ford's explanation, his only comment at its conclusion being, "You should have sent a courier to inform them who you were."

Zepeda's assurances of his good intentions caused Lee to use soft words. He told Zepeda that he accepted his promise "to pursue, apprehend, and punish" the outlaws found in Reynosa, and that he had ordered his own officers to assist him whenever it was necessary. Nevertheless, he feared that Zepeda was pretending and ordered Brackett to guard the American side of the Rio Grande, with Stoneman's squadron in support, to see that the Reynosans kept their promise. Recently he had heard that they had made threats against the residents of Edinburg and Tobasso, and Brackett was to give these towns adequate protection. Then, having made provision for the protection of the towns, Lee resumed his journey to Fort Brown.

Finally, at Brownsville, on April 12, Lee listened to many complaints and grievances from outraged residents. Out of them all came one alarming fact: both Mexican officials and citizens, covertly or openly, had aided Cortinas. Only six days earlier, General Guadalupe García had complained to Lee of Ford's occupation of Reynosa. This gave Lee an opportunity, in turn, to remind García of his border responsibilities, and that any shirking on his part might provoke even graver consequences. He had been told that Cortinas's confederates were in Matamoros planning to cross the Rio Grande to depredate in Brownsville. "If this is the case," he continued, "I shall expect, as an evidence of the friendly relations between the governments of the United States and Mexico, that they be apprehended and punished."

From García's reply, one may judge that he at least knew of such activities, but he affirmed that Mexican officials had always sought to adhere to strict American-

Mexican boundary agreements. When outlaws violated American friendship and trust, Mexican authorities had been prompt to mete out merited punishment. This had been a long-established policy, he said, although Mexico had been occupied with its own domestic problems. Yet, as an implied apology, seemingly, for the recent lack of energetic measures, he stated that the capital of Tamaulipas "was temporarily established at Tampico" and that the central government was "resident at Vera Cruz." In short, Mexico was in chaos, much as that part of it along the Rio Grande. He assured Lee, however, that he would vigorously seek out and lodge in jail those raiders within his jurisdiction.

Five days after Lee had received García's assurances, he wrote to Adjutant General Cooper his opinion of the Rio Grande situation. He was aware of the difficulty of defending small towns and isolated ranches on the United States' side of the river. The entire region from Eagle Pass to Brownsville was a vast, lonely mesquite-chaparral flat, with only occasional dim trails. It would require a force of 20,000 troops to police the region adequately. He repeated the professions of friendship of Mexican authorities and stated that they proposed strong measures to stamp out outlawry, but he felt that this could not be done because of unruly Mexicans who lived south of the border and who supported the Cortinas cause. He wrote Mrs. Lee that Mexican leaders lacked ability, but he remembered that the same statement could be made about Texans whose sympathies were with filibusters. "The last reliable account of Cortinas," he wrote, "was that he was retiring further into the interior of Mexico. He had with him his family and two men, and was more than one hundred miles from the frontier." Since April 11 Lee had insisted that García show evidence of his professed willingness to co-operate by action; and at last, he wrote, García had received orders to "arrest him [Cortinas] wherever found."

The defense of the western border of Texas against marauding Indians also gave Lee grave concern while he was at Brownsville. Several companies of troops formerly stationed at posts along this segment of the frontier had only recently been transferred to the Rio Grande. Their removal had brought a prompt protest from Governor Houston, who wanted Lee to induct Texas Rangers into federal service. Houston bluntly stated that the rangers were superior in every sense to federal soldiers and that they could well take care of the Indian problem. They were acquainted with Indian habits and mode of warfare and were woodsmen and marksmen. They knew where to find the Indians' haunts and how to trail and successfully pursue the raiders. Furthermore, he believed that they would act in defense of their homes, their families, and their neighbors, remembering the thousands of outrages the Indians had committed along the border. He argued that the Texans were hardy and could subsist on game, being dexterous hunters. "What are privations, suffering, and danger to them," he reasoned, "in comparison with the plaudits of their fellow-citizens, which follow their success." They were inured to the changing weather, to the heat of the prairies, to northers, and to violent storms. They were content with the earth for a bed and a blanket for a covering. Houston believed that with men like them on the border the marauders would keep their distance.

Houston painted a sordid picture of the border. The settlers in Palo Pinto and Eastland counties and the Germans along the Medina had only recently experienced the horrors of Indian raiders, who, indeed, had pillaged within thirty miles of San Antonio. "Not content with murdering the settlers and carrying off their horses," he complained, "they shoot the cattle in their path." Even now they were lurking in dense brakes and mountain fastnesses to make forays when the settlers were off guard. For this reason the settlers were deserting their cabins and their corn and wheat fields, and starvation stalked the land.

Lee recognized the justness of Houston's appeal, but he declined to accept the state troopers, promising that more vigorous measures would be taken immediately to aid the border people.

The month of May brought smiling skies, beautiful flowers, and green trees to Virginia but to Brownsville only blistering heat, and swarms of flies, mosquitoes, and fleas. Lee twiddled his thumbs, impatient to return to San Antonio so that he could work out more complete plans to combat the Indian raiding problem. By day his tormentors were flies and fleas, and by night, mosquitoes. "I have a lively time within doors," he wrote Mrs. Lee good-humoredly, "the fleas by day and the mosketoes by night. I am so extremely awkward at catching them that they mock at my effort."

When day after day had passed without reports of Mexican depredations, at last Lee made preparations to start for San Antonio. His wagons were greased, his mules foraged, and his men provisioned. Then came news of Cortinas. He had returned to Matamoros! Indolent *peones* threw off their listlessness to chatter and gesticulate as they collected in knots or surreptitiously carried the news from house to house. However, they were soon aware of a new order. Lee urged civil officials at Matamoros to seek Cortinas's arrest, but this move failed. Then he devised a plan to take him by surprise. He threw two columns of troops across the river to trap him, but evidently Mexican sympathizers had warned the bandit to leave, for the troopers did not find him.

This failure convinced Lee that he could do little else in Brownsville. Therefore, he instructed his officers to keep a strict watch along the Rio Grande and on May 6 started for San Antonio, 264 miles away. One week later, after an uneventful journey, he reached his headquarters.

In one respect Lee's visit to the Rio Grande was disappointing: Cortinas was yet at large. But in another it brought wholesome results: law and order returned to the Rio Grande; lawless Mexicans became more observant of citizens' rights; and Mexican officials promised co-operation in running down outlaws. The general morale of the settlers was appreciably higher than before Lee's visit. The sight of uniformed American troopers, carrying at their head the Stars and Stripes and riding fine, well-matched horses, was heartening. The federal troops had joined hands with the rangers to drive Cortinas and his gang far south of the border.

Lee knew, however, that the professions of Mexican officials and citizens was one thing and their actions another. Only recently Governor Houston's special commissioner, Robert H. Taylor, had written from Brownsville that Mexican officials knew of Cortinas's movements and allowed him to draw his "supplies of powder and ammunition from Matamoros."

Cortinas was yet the dashing outlaw, the Mexican of the hour, the Robin Hood of the *peones,* and a military and political figure of great power. Undoubtedly he would return to plague the border ranchos. That he continued to raid the lower Rio Grande Valley in later years, became a brigadier general in the Mexican Army, and was elected governor of Tamaulipas prove that he grew in the esteem of his worshipers. To Lee, however, he remained "that myth Cortinas"; but had Lee been allowed to deal with him in his own way, he would have been, as he expressed it, "a rough diplomatist, but a tolerably quick one."

★ IX ★

Camels and Comanches

BACK at San Antonio time ran swiftly, and Lee had little opportunity to relax. Official duties of directing the military activity of the department swamped him and limited the time available for writing home. Yet he did write a number of long-overdue letters.

These were troubled days, but San Antonio seemed hardly aware of events and little concerned, even with the heated slavery controversy then threatening to disrupt the Union. The listlessness of the Spanish Americans irked Lee. Indolently, they drove their clumsy, wooden-wheeled *carretas*, laden with vegetables, to the town markets or sold their produce on the streets; and whatever money their wares brought, they promptly spent without thought of the morrow. Some squatted idly by open jacal doorways, smoking *cigaretos* or watching the teeming life flow by; and still others strummed on guitars or engaged in frivolous pursuits, as though they had an eternity to live. Lee intensely disliked filth, and their hovels displayed it in variety, even though moderate improvements would have made them livable. And he cared little for their pastimes of horse racing, cockfighting, and dancing the bolero at the fandango or *baile* [ball]. In truth, he had no patience with idleness. To him, honest toil and industry were the symbols of progress.

His approval of these virtues he expressed in a letter to his son, Fitzhugh, shortly after his return to San Antonio. "I am glad to hear that your mechanics are all paid off," he began, "and that you have managed your funds so well as to have enough for your purposes. As you have commenced, I hope you will continue, never to exceed your means. It will save you much anxiety and mortification, and enable you to maintain your independence of character and feeling. It is easier to make our wishes conform to our means than to make our means conform to our wishes. In fact, we want but little. Our happiness depends upon our independence, the success of our operations, prosperity of our plans, health, contentment, and the esteem of our friends. All of which, my dear son, I hope you may enjoy."

From his experiences at Camp Cooper, Lee had every reason to conclude that Texas had an arid climate. At San Antonio little rain had fallen during the spring, and June brought drought and heat, with the mercury climbing above the 100-degree mark. San Antonio was insufferably hot. As though this were not enough of a handicap, Lee was boarding and "suffered all the annoyances" that a person of his "unfortunate temperament must undergo in such a country, and such a population." He expected no permanent stay in San Antonio because the ailing and venerable Brigadier General David E. Twiggs was due to relieve him of the command of the department.

Lee's only escape from the heat was to bathe in the cool San Antonio River, and, occasionally, to ride out into the country during the late hours of evening. He could not understand how the Spanish Americans lived in low-roofed hovels and went about their daily chores

Officers' Quarters, Quartermaster's Department, San Antonio

unaffected by the heat. Much of their activity seemed unnecessary to him. On June 25 he wrote Mrs. Lee that "Yesterday was St. John's Day" and "the principal or at least visible, means of adoration or worship seemed to consist in riding horses." It seemed to him that every Mexican who could procure "a quadruped" was cavorting through the streets, with the thermometer over a hundred degrees in the shade, a scorching sun, and dust several inches thick on the streets. He wondered at "the suffering of the horses, if not the pleasure of the riders," that "everything of the horse tribe had to be brought into requisition to accommodate the bipeds, unbroken colts and worn out hacks were saddled for the occasion. The plunging and kicking of the former procured excitement for, and the distress of the latter, merriment to the crowd. I did not know before that St. John set so high a value upon equitation."

Lee watched with interest the War Department's experiments with camels as beasts of burden at Camp Verde. He occasionally rode out to inquire how the tests were progressing. The officers in charge required the camels to travel with heavy loads for long distances through rough country and in all kinds of weather—blistering heat, snow, and rain. Up to the time of Lee's residence in San Antonio as department commander, they had met these tests well.

The most severe ordeal of this period had been to match them as carriers against mules in the Big Bend country. Army officials showed great interest and eagerly kept up with reports of camel exhibitions. On May 23, 1859, Lieutenant William H. Echols had left San Antonio with twenty-four camels and as many mules, all heavily laden, bound for Camp Hudson, the first stopping place on his journey. Every precaution had been taken to make the reconnaissance a success—an infantry company to guard against Indian attack, kegs filled with water and carried on camels' backs, and sundry other supplies. The female camels had carried burdens of 300 pounds and the male camels of 500 pounds. From Camp Hudson, Echols moved through desolate, barren country to Fort Davis, down into deep canyons, over rough mountains, across arid plateaus, and through dense chaparral and mesquite jungles. Occasionally the mules made better progress than the camels and were more sure-footed over slippery ground in rainy weather or in crossing streams. On the other hand, the camels were not distressed to go two or three days without water and could stand the heat and strain of dry weather better.

Lee wanted more positive proofs of the feasibility of using camels. Certainly the camels had proved their usefulness as beasts of burden, but in many respects mules had met equally well the demands of the recent reconnaissance. Secretary Floyd felt the same need for additional trials and ordered Lee to continue the experiment. On May 31, 1860, therefore, Lee ordered Echols to make a second trip to the Rio Grande. On this reconnaissance he was to make a wide, looping sweep between Camp Hudson and Fort Davis, reaching as far south as the Rio Grande, through a much more arid and broken country; and when he arrived at the Rio Grande, he was to locate a site for a military post near the Comanche Trail. He was furnished with twenty camels and fifteen pack mules and all the necessary supplies. As on the previous expedition, the camels carried barrels of water and sundry other materials. Lee wrote his daughter, Agnes, that he thought it a pity that they could "not partake of what they carry for others." But this, of course, was a part of the test.

Once more infantry was to prove its worth under a terrible ordeal. Second Lieutenant J. H. Holman, with thirty-one privates from the First Infantry, accompanied Echols as an escort. Well-equipped men, heavily burdened camels trudging along in six detachments, and a train of mules left San Antonio, headed west, to undergo the most severe trials for both man and beast yet undertaken.

From Camp Hudson, on June 24, Echols and his party struck out toward the southwest, across a region of no roads and only Indian and wild-game trails. At the Pecos, he left his former route to his right, traveling in a southwesterly direction across a dry wilderness broken by mountains, dry arroyos, canyons, buttes, and plains. Echols's most persistent and annoying worry was that he was entering a region of little or no water, and it was desperately hot. The sun beat down mercilessly on the toiling men and beasts. Under the conditions they required water at frequent intervals, if they were not to suffer. But Echols knew that it was not to be had, for the drought had dried up even the few water holes usually found in this country.

For four days, 120 miles, the expedition stumbled on through this desolate region. Up precipitous mountainsides, down into deep canyons, through brush, over boulder-strewn terrain, and across eroded mesas, Echols rationed the water carefully to the men and the mules. For two days the camels seemed not to thirst. Then they, too, showed the strain, in that at night they would not graze or sleep. By July 2 the crisis was reached. There was only enough water left to give each man a drink, without any for the mules or camels. Echols told his men of their desperate plight. They could not expect to reach Fort Stockton or the Rio Grande, and certainly the Pecos was too far away. They must find water, even though a stagnant pool, nearer their line of march. After they had drunk their last water, they would disperse to search for a pool, and if it were not found, they would make their way out of the country as best they could. Echols's journal for this day portrays their suffering in dramatic terms.

"Marched westwardly most of the day," it ran, "and after a long march of 29.4 miles over a rough country, camped dry without any prospects of finding water, in about the poorest prospect of making progress I have ever been situated. We were all very uneasy, not to say a little frightened, for our welfare. The mules must go without water to-night, are broken down now, and some are expected to be abandoned on the march to-morrow. We have only water sufficient for the men thirty hours, the Pecos, Rio Grande, and Fort Stockton, are too distant to reach, which we expected to attain, we may be unable to reach from the impassibility of the region. Our march today has been rough, and too rough tomorrow, I fear, for many lives that are now with us to stem. The animals go to the barrels and draw the bungs with their teeth and gnaw at the bung holes. The second time in my life I have seen a quart of water priceless, almost. We have sent a man to search for water, to be paid liberally if he succeeds; if not, all the mules we expect to lose."

Under a blazing sun, presently entirely without water,

the men and beasts trudged on wearily, with little hope of relief. Again, on the night of July 3, they made a dry camp, but no one could rest or sleep. Burning thirst consumed all. Mules had fallen by the wayside during the day, and even the camels showed dire distress, but no one could think of stopping, for to linger was death.

At the next dawn they were on the move. They were now at the end of their resources. Then Echols spied in the distance an oddly shaped mountain, Camel's Hump! They were saved if only they could reach it, for at its foot were springs of cold water that fed San Francisco Creek! But it was many weary miles away. When he gave this news to the suffering men, it spurred them on to superhuman effort. Now all eyes were fixed on this beacon of hope as though it might become a mirage, soon to fade away.

"No one can imagine the feeling of a thirsty man till he sees one," Echols wrote. "I would not describe it by vain attempt, as vain almost as that would be which I might use in describing the region of country just passed over which made them so; a region in its original chaotic state, as if the progress of civilization was too rapid for the arrangement of chaos; a picture of barrenness and desolation, when the scathing fire of destruction has swept with its rabid flame mountains, canons, ravines, precipices, castus, soap-weed, intense reflection from the limestone cliffs, and almost every barrier that one can conceive of to make an impossibility to progress."

As the plodding men and animals came within two or three miles of San Francisco Creek, all order vanished, and they ran madly toward water. The thirsty, suffering beasts had smelled it. Wildly they plunged into its sparkling depths, the men laughing and shouting, drinking their fill and pouring the precious liquid over their heads and bodies. Never before had life been so sweet! This was the Fourth of July, and they celebrated it boisterously. All else was forgotten in their delirium of joy.

The remainder of the journey was without incident, although the country was just as rough and desolate. Nature had seemingly cut jagged gashes across barren limestone mountains, leaving precipices hundreds of feet deep, buttes and peaks of fantastic shapes, and deep arroyos and canyons blocked here and there by huge boulders. But at least there was water, and the soldiers seemed not to mind the rugged country. From San Francisco Creek they made their way to Fort Davis, where both men and beasts could find food and rest. On July 12 they were on the march again, southward toward the Rio Grande, their route being along an uncertain road from Fort Davis to Presidio del Norte. From the latter place they traveled over a rugged mountain country to Lates Lengua, and down its valley to the Rio Grande, where Echols sought to find a site for a military post, as he had been instructed. Finding no suitable place, he moved on down the river for twenty miles below the Comanche Trail crossing, where at last he found one. A post here could be supplied by building a wagon road along the San Carlos Trail and coming into the Comanche Trail near Camel's Hump Mountain, although such a road would have a serious obstacle—a precipitous mountainside, rocky and several hundred feet high.

Echols presently completed his reconnaissance without further mishap, redistributing his men, beasts, and equipment at Camps Hudson and Verde. His expedition had been a brilliant success and had proven the superiority of camels as beasts of burden. Lee had not expected that the men would encounter such a gruelling experience, but he was impressed and pleased with their success in spite of it. He wrote to Adjutant General Cooper "of camels, whose endurance, docility, and sagacity will not fail to attract the attention of the Secretary of War, and but for whose reliable services the reconnaissance would have failed."

During the weeks of Echols's reconnaissance, Lee's interest had been divided. Although he was very much interested in the camel experiment, his thoughts had turned uneasily toward the Indian country. Every day brought fresh news of Indian forays. Governor Houston continued to insist that the border was in desolation, listing 51 persons killed, as many more taken prisoner, 1,800 horses stolen, and much property destroyed. He had again urged Lee to accept the use of state troops in the emergency, but his offer was again politely declined.

In the almost three years since Lee had ridden away from Camp Cooper for the last time, many Indian raids had occurred, centering about this post. It will be recalled that Lee had referred to Camp Cooper as a "desert of dullness"; but within a few months after his departure, the "desert" was no longer dull.

In August, 1858, a notoriously "bad Indian" (Penateka Comanche), Santa Anna, with a Naconi warrior, had stopped at the Comanche reserve on his way to steal horses from the near-by settlers. Katumse had ordered him to leave, but he had refused. Then Agent Leeper had called upon Lieutenant Cornelius Van Camp to use his Camp Cooper troopers to expel the visiting Indians. Van

Camp had hastened up with his nineteen enlisted men, all he had at the post. Learning this, seventy of Katumse's warriors and their women and children, thinking that the soldiers intended to massacre them all, also came— all armed with rifles and bows and arrows—and angrily threatened to attack the soldiers unless they withdrew immediately. Van Camp ignored the threats and gave orders for his men to enter the house in which the outlaw Indians were hiding.

The excited Indians then prepared to carry out their threats. Katumse pleaded with them not to attack the soldiers, saying that they were there to drive away the "bad men" and not to harm the reservation Indians. But his "talk" was in vain. One of his subchiefs, Tosh-e-weh, who acted for the rebels, warned Katumse and his white friends that "he, every man, woman and child would die rather than see these men killed."

This only angered Katumse the more. "Too much talk, no good," he growled as he sprang forward to enter the house after the visiting Indians. But he was violently seized and restrained by about thirty squaws, who in tears begged him not to cause trouble.

Still thoroughly aroused, Katumse next called upon all his loyal tribesmen to line up beside him, Leeper, and Van Camp. Only his brother, a nephew, an old Indian named "Hawk," and two others joined him. At this juncture, the sergeant in charge of the troopers informed Van Camp that he had discovered that he had only one round of ammunition and that there was no more back at the post. Van Camp was thunderstruck. One round of ammunition and all about the imperiled soldiers were howling, angry Indians! With no other alternative, he ordered his men to return to the post. Undoubtedly he would have pressed his attempted arrest of the two Indians, even in the face of overwhelming odds, had he not been faced with this drastic handicap.

That evening Tosh-e-weh and a body of select warriors called on Leeper, determined to kill him. But his firm yet kind reception caused them to change their minds. They told him that their previous hostile threat had been dictated by a rumor that the soldiers had been given orders to massacre all the Indians. He assured them that this was not true, that he and Van Camp were still their friends. And he permitted Tosh-e-weh to escort the visiting Indians away from the reservation to guarantee that they would not be harmed.

This incident greatly emboldened the wild Comanches to use the reservation on their way to and from the Texas frontier settlements to steal horses. More than once the angry settlers had followed their trails to the reservation and had found their stolen horses there. Each time, however, Katumse had assured the white men that neither he nor his people were responsible for these thefts and had returned the stolen animals. As the raids increased, so did the demands of the settlers that the federal government abandon the reservation experiment and move the Indians back across the Red River. John R. Baylor, who was the Comanche agent while Lee was at Camp Cooper and who had been dismissed from the Indian Service because of a quarrel with Supervising Agent Neighbors, led this settler movement.

In May, 1859, Major Thomas reported that Baylor had brought 250 armed men to the reservation to attack the Indians but that Camp Cooper troops had driven them away. The settlers had skirmished with the Comanches and then had withdrawn to Martin's Ranch. The angry Indians followed them and engaged them in a running fight, in which six whites and three warriors were killed. This affair fired the whole border with a spirit of revenge, and soon armed frontiersmen camped about the reservation and kept Thomas's garrison on the alert.

Greatly concerned, Governor Houston now sent commissioners to investigate; and when the angry settlers refused to give testimony, the commissioners, hearing only the Agency version, finally endorsed the reservation policy. The settlers straightway held meetings in their border towns and communities to protest to the Governor and the President. And at last, in August, 1859, the Commissioner of Indian Affairs ordered the abandonment of the reservation. Thus, defeated and despondent, Neighbors rounded up his reservation charges, and Thomas furnished him an escort to march them safely across the Red River. Neighbors was killed at Fort Belknap a short time later by a "border tough."

These disturbing events had occurred while General Twiggs was in command of the department and before Lee had returned from his prolonged leave in Virginia. Twiggs had admitted that the federal policy toward the wild Indians was defensive and had written General Scott for authority to send his cavalry far within the Indian country to seek out and destroy the raiders' villages. Only then, he thought, might the Indians "let Texas alone."

Already Texas Rangers and Brazos Agency Indians under Ford and Agent Ross had set a pattern for him. They had struck a large Kotsoteka village on Little Robe

Creek, north of the Canadian, in Indian Territory, and had killed seventy-six warriors and had taken eighteen prisoners, mostly women and children. This was the most crushing defeat the Indians had ever suffered at the hands of their white foes, and had forced the survivors to ask for peace and the right to settle down on a reservation.

Secretary Floyd had approved Twiggs's proposal for offensive warfare, for which the Second Cavalry was to become the spearhead. Since Major Thomas was the ranking officer of this regiment during Lee's absence in Virginia, he naturally expected to lead any expedition sent against the Indians. He felt considerably crestfallen when Twiggs favored Van Dorn and objected strenuously, charging that Twiggs had ignored his rights, and appealed directly to Secretary Floyd. He asked that a court of inquiry be named to look into the matter. This nettled the garrulous Twiggs, who reproved Thomas for his "uncourteousness" in going over his head. Thomas fired back just as heatedly, twitting him for his bad grammar and stating boldly that Lee would have recognized his rights had he been in Texas. Fortunately, no harm resulted from this quarrel, and Van Dorn was permitted to proceed on his way.

He moved northward with a strong cavalry force, assisted by Ross and his Brazos Agency Indian trailers. From Camp Cooper, in the fall of 1859, he crossed into Indian Territory and established Camp Radziminski, on Otter Creek. And while he was yet improving his position, his trailers brought in a report that a large band of Comanches was camping near the Wichita village, about ninety miles to the east, near present-day Rush Springs.

Van Dorn sounded "Boots and Saddles," and the troopers were away within an hour.

Thirty-six hours later they attacked and destroyed the village of 120 lodges and killed fifty-eight Comanches, suffering a loss among themselves of Lieutenant Van Camp, one sergeant, and three enlisted men.

This Comanche defeat was heralded among western army men as a brilliant victory. But it proved to be a costly blunder and caused serious repercussions in Washington, for Interior Department officials charged that the border army had frustrated their peace plans. This band of Comanches was on its way to Fort Arbuckle to attend a peace council at the invitation of Commandant Powell. Obviously, the Indians would later view any peace proposal of their white foes with suspicion. News of the Comanche disaster spread like a prairie fire, inducing most of the wild tribes to seek the safety of the deep canyons of the High Plains and some to cross the Rio Grande into Mexico.

During the next year, on April 13, after Lee had assumed command of the department, Van Dorn followed up this success by moving again from Radziminski to strike Buffalo Hump's village on a small creek south of old Fort Atkinson, in Kansas. Almost the entire band was wiped out, and its chief barely escaped with his life.

But Twiggs's offensive operations had not brought peace to the Texas border. Instead, the raids of the Comanches and the Kiowas were only intensified. These Indians had leagued with the Arapahoes and the Cheyennes, farther north, to wage implacable warfare on the white man wherever he might be found—in Texas, in Kansas, in Colorado, or in New Mexico. They saw their enemies pressing in on every side. The Five Civilized Tribes of Indian Territory were advancing from the east; the whites in Kansas, Colorado, and New Mexico, from the north and west; and other whites, the Texans, from the south. If they were to preserve their hunting grounds and maintain their nomadic customs, they must wage ceaseless war. The treatment of Katumse's Comanches at Camp Cooper had convinced them that they had no other course to pursue.

This, then, was the Indian problem Lee had inherited from his predecessor. But he attacked it immediately. His answer to Governor Houston's appeal for border protection was to inaugurate the most active scouting service the border had yet seen. Generally, his patrols met no Indians and returned to their posts empty-handed; but some engaged in skirmishes and were successful. Lee's subordinates were inspired by his earnest determination, for he would not ask them to do anything for which he had not already set the pattern. Consequently, by October 30, 1860, they had reported nine successes against raiding Indians, and in his Special Order No. 16, of this date, Lee reported these encouraging results.

Two of these affairs proved the mettle of both the pursuers and the pursued. The first was when Lee's nephew, Second Lieutenant Fitzhugh Lee, left Camp Colorado on the afternoon of January 15, 1860, in pursuit of a small band of Indian raiders seen driving a herd of stolen horses up Pecan Bayou, in Brown County. Young Lee pressed his pursuit and soon overtook two of the marauders, who were impeded in their flight because of having to drive their stolen horses before them. Lee's men killed one of the Indians; but the other, mounted on a fast horse, managed to outdistance them. Lieutenant Lee, also being well mounted, gave chase.

"The chase led over hills and ravines covered with dense cedar for six or seven miles," the department commander's citation ran, "when the Indian, hard-pressed, attempted to escape on foot. Lieutenant Lee dismounted, and after a search of several hours, came suddenly upon him and killed him in a personal combat. All the animals, twenty-four were captured." This recital is devoid of the color and intense drama that must have been present. In fact, many years later Captain George F. Price of the Fifth Cavalry added interesting details. He said that young Fitzhugh Lee found the Indian hiding in a thicket behind a ledge of rock and rushed upon him. The next moment they were locked in deadly, hand-to-hand combat. One of young Lee's men, Bugler Hayes, rushed up to shoot the Indian but could not for fear of hitting his superior. Finally, Lee threw his foe by a "back-heel" fall and killed him.

Colonel Lee's old friend, Major Thomas, headed the second expedition. On July 23, with a small unit of the Second Cavalry, including his musicians and three scouts, he left Camp Cooper to reconnoiter the headwaters of the Colorado and the Concho, traveling over the Butterfield Trail via Phantom Hill and through Mountain Pass to the Colorado River. Here Lieutenant Lee, with a company of the Second Cavalry from Camp Colorado, joined him, and the march was resumed. As they were moving up the Middle Concho, they were joined by Captain Richard W. Johnson and still a third company of the Second Cavalry from Fort Mason, bringing Thomas's combined force to more than one hundred men. They scouted thoroughly the region now embraced in Sterling, Glasscock, Irion, Tom Green, and Reagan and parts of Mitchell and Howard counties, but without success. Not a human being was seen, except the station agents of the stage line, who told the soldiers that they had heard of no Indians near their posts that summer.

Learning this, Thomas ordered Johnson and Lee to return their troopers to their home posts, and he turned back over the stage road for Camp Cooper. He had reached a point beyond Mountain Pass when Doss, a Delaware scout, came in with a report that he had cut an Indian trail twenty-five miles farther west. Thomas quickly ordered pursuit, taking about twenty mounted men and pack mules with him and sending his wagon train on to Camp Cooper.

The hard-riding troopers covered more than forty miles before they stopped to rest, and at daybreak the next morning they were off again. Ultimately they reached a point on the Salt Fork of the Brazos about sixty miles from where they had struck the trail.

There, from the top of a small butte, Doss looked into the distance. "There they are!" he shouted, pointing to a small Indian encampment about one mile ahead.

There indeed were eleven Comanches, with a herd of horses grazing near by. The Indians sighted their pursuers and leaped on their ponies to leave. Thomas could not charge them, for a deep ravine intervened, and while his men in single file were crossing it by following a buffalo trail, the Indians were rapidly making their escape.

The Comanches were slowed down by their horse herd, however, and the troopers overtook them rapidly.

The Indians had gained "some distance," Lee's report ran, "but after a chase of four miles, were pressed so closely that they abandoned their animals and took to flight. One warrior, more resolute than the rest kept his position in the rear of the party, when, suddenly dismounting, he faced his pursuers, determined to sacrifice himself for his comrades' safety. The troops pressed upon him too eagerly, and several of his arrows took effect, before he fell, pierced by twenty balls."

When Thomas saw that the Indian was wounded, although the Indian had wounded him, he directed Doss to ask him in his own language if he would surrender, and that if he would, his life would be spared. To this query, the proud old Comanche replied: "Surrender? Never! Never! Come on!"

Major Thomas was wounded in the chin and the chest. Private William Murphy, of Company D, was disabled by a kick from his horse. Lee wrote of the affair later that, seeing this, "the dying Indian rushed upon him [Murphy] with his lance, but had only strength to inflict a slight wound. Chief Bugler Hausser also received a lance wound in his chest. The rest of the Indians, mounted on fresh and fleet horses, escaped; the cavalry horses having been completely exhausted by the long and rapid pursuit. Twenty-eight horses were captured."

Troops from Camp Cooper, Lee's former "Texas home," were to share in yet another Indian fight during this year. In December, shortly before Lee was relieved of the department command, a large raiding party of Naconi Comanches, under their great chief, Peta Nacona, had descended on the northwestern Texas frontier to secure horses and plunder for trade with the New Mex-

Nimitz Hotel, Fredericksburg, Texas

ican *Comancheros* encamped on the headwaters of the Canadian. Quickly L. S. Ross, afterwards to become a Texas governor, started in pursuit with 136 men, including Sergeant Spangler and 13 troopers of the Second Cavalry. They found the trail of the marauders above Camp Cooper and followed it up to the broken country of the Pease River, north of present-day Crowell, above the confluence of the Pease and Mule Creek, and attacked the unsuspecting Indians before they could make defense preparations. The Naconies leaped on their horses and fled wildly, with the yelling white men in hot pursuit.

Ross singled out Peta Nacona, overtook him, and killed him in a spirited duel. Lieutenant Thomas Kelliher pursued another Indian, and after a race of two miles he drew near enough to fire. As he raised his rifle with this intention, the supposed warrior stopped and faced him, holding forth a child. It proved to be a white woman, who revealed her identity by shouting to him, *"Americano! Americano!"* She willingly returned with Kelliher to camp.

The woman only shook her head when later Ross sought to ply her with questions concerning her identity. She could not understand English. Ross believed that she was Cynthia Ann Parker, who had been captured by the Indians almost twenty-five years before, whose anxious kinsmen had made more than one vain attempt to ransom her from the Indians. So he sent a runner to Birdville, near present-day Fort Worth, to inform the venerable Isaac Parker, Cynthia Ann's uncle, that he was returning to Camp Cooper with a captive woman who might be his niece.

When Ross and his force returned to Camp Cooper,

Mrs. Evans, the wife of Commandant N. G. Evans, cared for the captured woman and child, although it was necessary to place a guard about the house in which the captives were held to prevent the woman from escaping.

Upon the arrival of Isaac Parker, the captive woman was brought before him. The old man sought to talk with her through an interpreter but could gain no satisfaction. Finally, in bitter disappointment, he turned toward Captain Ross and expressed his doubts that this was Cynthia Ann. Immediately the startled woman began patting her breast, saying "Cynthia Ann! Cynthia Ann!" A ray of recollection dormant for twenty-five years had sprung up in her mind. Parker stated later that "Her very countenance changed and a pleasant smile took the place of a sullen gloom."

Cynthia Ann returned with her uncle to his home in Tarrant County. For a time she could not adapt herself to white men's ways, so long had she lived among the Indians, but finally she became accustomed to them. Her child, Topasannah, or "Prairie Flower," died in 1864; and a few years after the Civil War the mother followed her to the grave.

Ross's expedition brought down the curtain on Comanche campaigns under the direction of Lee as department commander.

At San Antonio hot August dragged out its weary length. Then at last came moisture-laden Gulf breezes, bringing rain and lower temperatures. Lee's spirits revived. In the past changes of this sort had brought more than one quip from him. On August 22 he wrote his daughter, Annie, telling her of the rain and inviting her to visit him in San Antonio. If she would come, he would buy her a fine horse and even accompany her about town in a wagon, whenever that was necessary. But, he warned teasingly, "Our flies and mosquitoes are re-animated," although they could be endured better than the heat in which for the last several weeks San Antonio's "Shadracks, Mesheks and Abednigos" had sweltered.

Lee's remaining weeks there were spent pleasantly. He took great interest in sponsoring the building of St. Mark's Episcopal Church and in its services. Frequently he dined with friends, bouncing their small children on his knee or entertaining them with stories and light-hearted banter. But there were times when the conversation would turn to slavery, disunion, and abolition fanaticism; and with troubled mien he would express his anxiety, fear, and pessimism.

At last, on December 13, Twiggs arrived, and Lee was relieved of the command of the Department of Texas. He could now leave his desk and ride away to rejoin his regiment at Fort Mason to share in the rough-and-tumble life of the border. There, at least for a short time, he could turn his eyes from the ominous storm of secession rapidly approaching and seek release for his restless spirit on the frontier. Six days later he paid all his debts, took leave of his friends, and rode out toward the northwest.

Farewell to Texas

ONCE more the vagaries of Texas weather brought discomfort to Lee. At San Antonio during the summer of 1860 the heat had been searing, bringing long and trying days. Now, in December, on the road to Fort Mason a cold norther blew in, with ice and freezing rain festooning the bushes and trees and giving the forest the appearance of a fairyland. Camping by the roadside brought little relief or rest; and when Lee rode on, his horse's footing was uncertain and progress was slow. Hour after hour he faced the sharp wind until it seemed to pierce his heavy woolen coat. He was cold and miserable until he arrived at the post on Saturday, December 23, in time to join his friends in their Christmas festivities. The warm fires, the tables loaded with food and drink, Christmas trees bending with gifts and draped with tinsel, music, laughter, and good cheer—all carried his thoughts over eighteen hundred miles to Arlington, where Christmas was again being celebrated without him. Lee had ridden into a new world; hence for this day he tried to banish his fears for the Union and his anxiety on account of his family and to enjoy the hospitality and comforts of his friends.

This was Fort Mason's slack season, for Indian raiders, with the exception of those who moved up from camps in Mexico, seldom braved the wintry blasts to leave their villages for protracted periods. Ordinarily they preferred their retreats in the deep canyons of the Staked Plains or in river valleys, protected by a north bank. Snug in their lodges, they could live off of jerked meat or food stolen from the settlers and plan for the coming year. Army officers seasoned in border warfare were well aware of this custom of the Indians; so, feeling that there was little danger of immediate attack, the Fort Mason commander allowed his troopers to stoke their campfires and enjoy Christmas.

The officers' families vied with each other in entertaining Lee, who was always a favorite, particularly with the children. They would sit by the fireside far into the night listening to his tales and watching the firelight play on his face. At one moment his eyes might be grave and sad, but at another they would light with faith and gaiety. He interested young and old alike with his stories of Mexican War days, of his family, and of West Point. But when the talk of the elders turned to national affairs, his voice became vibrant with emotion. In his every mood could be sensed his nobility of character, his lofty idealism, and his faith in an overruling Providence.

Lee always returned social courtesies promptly and was a conscientious host. Soon he had an additional incentive for hospitality. On January 22 his new adjutant, Lieutenant William Warren Lowe, arrived from St. Louis with his young bride. Lee entertained them at breakfast. For the occasion, Billy, his cook and handy man, brought out his very best "equipage" from his mess chest and set before the young couple an appetizing meal. Later in the day Lee wrote humorously about the occa-

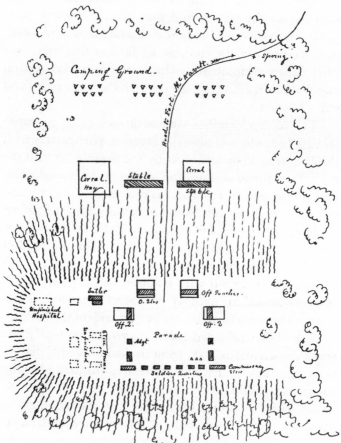

Fort Mason at the time of Colonel Joseph K. F. Mansfield's
inspection tour of the Texas
border posts in 1857

sion to Mrs. Lee's cousin, "Markie" [Martha Custis Williams]. "What is your conception of a bridal breakfast in the Comanche country?" he asked. " . . . the most important accompaniment is a fine appetite." He added, "The lady's, I am sorry to say, was timid, her swain's, bold and soldiery, and he attacked the beef steak, hashed turkey and boiled eggs fearlessly. They dine today with their left hand neighbor and come to me again tomorrow."

This was the first time that Lee had entertained in style, although he wrote his wife that he had some ladies and gentlemen to breakfast with him before—Mr. and Mrs. Shaaf, on the morning of their departure, and Dr. and Mrs. Engle, when they were passing by.

Occasionally, Lee's thoughts turned to his own military situation. Now fifty-four years of age, he was only a lieutenant colonel. He had been twenty-two years advancing from the rank of captain to his present rating, and his gross income was only $4,060, including his salary of $1,205 and allowances for rations, quarters, travel, and other expenses. This was hardly sufficient to meet his own simple needs and the greater requirements of his family, beyond those met by their private income. He found little comfort in the fact that there were no immediate prospects of a new brigadier general, for even if there were, many other officers had higher rank. Only recently Secretary Floyd had sponsored a brigadier generalship for Lee's Mexican War comrade, Joseph E. Johnston, to whom Lee wrote his hearty congratulations. Still he unquestionably felt that he had been forgotten. All he could do for himself was to ask his son, Custis, to put in an oar for him if another chance should arise.

Try as he might, Lee could not stop his ears to the rising mutterings of dissension that was threatening to disrupt the Union; nor could his fellow officers—Thomas, Stoneman, Oakes, Van Dorn, Hood, and others. They, too, were West Pointers with army careers before them. They anxiously watched their grave-faced commander and talked in guarded language about current issues. What would Lee do, and, indeed, what would they do, if civil war should come?

Lincoln's election as president of the United States had caused South Carolina to lead three other southern states into secession, and throughout the North and East were heard threats of coercing them back into the Union. Still vacillating, President Buchanan floundered in a sea of indecision, refusing to send food and men to Fort Moultrie in Charleston Harbor to strengthen its federal garrison for fear that he would bring on war. In December the aging J. J. Crittenden, attempting to play Henry Clay's role of Great Compromiser, presented to the United States Senate six amendments and four resolutions designed to ease the tension. He proposed to give legal protection to slaveowners, to guarantee to them federal compensation for escaped slaves, and to extend the 36° 30′–line of the Missouri Compromise to the Pacific. But a Senate committee to consider the proposals failed to approve them; and, similarly, a House committee of thirty-three members later reported that it could arrive at no compromise.

Worriedly, on January 23 Lee wrote his wife his misgivings. He had read and enjoyed Everett's *Life of Washington,* which she had sent him, but he could not help but think how the spirit of this great man would grieve if he could see the wreck of his mighty labors. He yet had faith that his countrymen would sustain the Union. "I will not permit myself to believe," he declared, "till all ground for hope is gone, that the work of his noble deeds will be destroyed, and that his precious advice and virtuous example will soon be forgotten by his countrymen." Lee had also scanned New Orleans newspapers, hoping to allay his fears and anxiety, but instead he found a nation delicately poised on the brink of "anarchy and civil war." "May God avert us from both," he wrote feelingly. "I fear mankind for years will not be sufficiently Christianized to bear the absence of restraint and force. I see that four States have declared themselves out of the Union. Four more apparently will follow their example. Then if the border States are dragged into the gulf of revolution, one half of the country will be arrayed against the other, and I must try and be patient and wait the end, for I can do nothing to hasten or retard it." Here on a remote frontier, Lee must have paced the floor of his hut in deep agitation, for indeed there was nothing he could do to affect the final decision.

Five days later he again wrote on the same subject. He had learned that the Crittenden proposals had failed and was disappointed. "They were fair and just," he said. "The action of the Southern States in seizing public property and capturing United States forts will not calm the angry feelings of the country. If the bond of the Union can only be maintained by the sword and the bayonet instead of brotherly love and friendship, and if strife and civil war are to take the place of mutual aid and commerce, its existence will lose all interest to me." Against such an eventuality he expressed his hope in the wisdom and patriotism of the nation and the overruling Providence of a merciful God. Since Virginia had led in the movement to draw up the Constitution, "so I would wish," he concluded, "that she might be able to maintain it to save the Union." Already Texas had called a convention to consider secession, which, if approved, might make it necessary for Lee to withdraw the Second Cavalry beyond the Red River.

National events moved with dramatic swiftness. On the day after Christmas, Major Anderson, under verbal orders from the Secretary of War, had spiked Fort Moultrie's guns and had, over the protests of South Carolina, moved his small garrison to the more easily defended Fort Sumter, out in the harbor. Between January 1 and February 1, 1861, Mississippi, Florida, Alabama, Georgia, Louisiana, and Texas passed the ordinances of secession; and on February 4 the Confederate States of America was formed at Montgomery, Alabama. Its provisional congress elected Jefferson Davis of Mississippi president, and later, in May, named Richmond the permanent capital.

Lee watched with great anguish of spirit this threatening storm. Even at his border post there were concrete indications of brewing trouble. Suspicious-looking men lurked about Fort Mason, and Lee called on Captain Richard W. Johnson one day and asked him whether he could rely upon his support if Fort Mason were attacked. Johnson replied, "Yes, so long as I hold a commission in the Union army." Pleased, Lee then told Johnson of his plans to fortify the post; but on February 13 Scott's Order No. 16 reached him, requiring that he give up his field command and return to Washington immediately. Lee prepared to depart at once, paying his debts and distributing his "little valuables among the officers."

"Colonel, do you intend to go South or remain North?" Captain Johnson asked Lee as he was climbing into his ambulance to leave.

"I shall never bear arms against the United States—but it may be necessary for me to carry a musket in defense of my native state, Virginia," was his reply.

The driver cracked his whip, and the ambulance lurched forward. Lee thrust his head out of his hack and shouted back, "Good-by! God bless you!"

Although Lee's stay at Fort Mason had been brief, he left devoted friends. In later years both civilians and soldiers spoke highly of him and told of his visits to their homes. A captain of the Second Cavalry, who later fought against Lee, said that he "was one of the most agreeable men I ever knew, handsome, courteous as a knight, pleasant and entertaining in conversation. He was universally beloved by all the officers of his regiment."

Settlers about the post remembered him as courteous, simple, and wholesome, with native dignity, gentle and unobtrusive, yet singularly commanding. One said that he was full of affability and small talk to the ladies, but that one could not be in his presence without an instinctive feeling that he was "one of the greatest of men." Another said: "I never saw Lee but once, but he made an impression upon me I cannot forget. He was standing upon the gallery of the government building in San Antonio, watching a squad of infantry that were being drilled by a lieutenant. His appearance was so impressive that I stopped to look at him and ask who he was. There was a remarkable repose about him, singularly in contrast with the group of officers about him. He seemed a column of antique marble, a pillar of state—so calm, so serene, so thoughtful, and so commanding! I stood within a few feet of him, perhaps five minutes, and during the time he did not once open his lips. The conviction possessed me at once, and I said involuntarily to myself: 'There stands a great man!' "

At a well-known spring beside the San Antonio road, Lee met and had lunch with another young friend, Captain George Blake Cosby. "I told him that General Scott wanted to consult with him as to a campaign against the seceded States," Cosby wrote many years later. "He feared so, too; that Virginia had seceded and war was certain. As he said this, he showed more emotion than is recorded of him when he had won or lost a great battle later on. He told me if he found my surmises correct he would tender his resignation and offer his services to his native State."

After Lee's noonday conversation with Captain Cosby, he rode on toward San Antonio, greatly troubled in mind. What would he do if Virginia joined the Confederacy? Should he, too, take his stand with the Confederacy? Or should he resign his commission and retire to private life? For the remainder of his journey, these questions must have harrassed him.

San Antonio seethed with excitement when Lee's ambulance drew up in front of the Read House. Its streets were swarmed with grim-visaged men wearing red insignia on their coats or shirts. A correspondent to the Austin *State Gazette* described the scene a few hours after Lee's arrival. "Eight o'clock Saturday, morning," he wrote. "Our usually quiet city is full of soldiers. All the important streets are guarded, and the main plaza looks like a vast military camp."

Lee felt gravely alarmed, although he must have known that something like this might occur at any time. "Who are these men?" he asked a Mrs. Caroline Darrow, whom he met near the stage. "They are McCulloch's," she explained. "General Twiggs surrendered everything to the state this morning, and we are all prisoners of war."

Lee was startled out of his usual self-composure by this dramatic statement, and he made further inquiry. He was told that soon after Twiggs had succeeded him as department commander, he had revealed his Southern sympathies in letters to the Adjutant General. As the Texas secession crisis approached, he asked his superiors for instructions, but none were given. Then he wanted to be relieved of his command, and Colonel Carlos A. Waite was sent to succeed him.

Before Waite arrived, however, Twiggs surrendered to Colonel Ben McCulloch all federal arms, munitions, properties, and military posts under his command. It was agreed that Twiggs's San Antonio garrison of 160 men should evacuate and surrender all local federal properties to the Committee of Public Safety, that the troops should retain their sidearms and camp and garrison equipage, and that all the federal posts in the state should be turned over to the state of Texas, the troops to march to the coast for embarkation. Twiggs agreed to these terms on February 18. Acting for the committee, Henry E. McCulloch took over the northern Texas posts, and John S. Ford, the southern.

Waite sought to repudiate the surrender agreement when he arrived, but it was too late. The Clarksville *Standard* of March 9, 1861, carrying a San Antonian's narrative of events dated February 18, said: "He [Waite] rode up to the Alamo building, but seeing the Lone Star flag flying from its summit, turned off, after a hurried conversation with a regular on the inside, entered a neighboring grocery, and smiled his grief away." Indeed, Waite's opposition only led to his own arrest by the Texans and to the holding of his men as prisoners of war.

After his talk with Mrs. Darrow, Lee went to his hotel room, attired himself as a private citizen, and then walked over to his old headquarters to learn more about what had happened. To his surprise Texans representing the Committee of Public Safety—Samuel A. Maverick, Thomas Devine, and Phillip N. Luckett— were in charge. They accepted his salutation with reserve and bluntly told him that Texas was out of the Union and had become a Confederate state and that he must also declare himself for the new cause.

This was Lee's first severe test of loyalty. The Texans' demand that he support the new order shocked his sense of propriety. He was yet an officer of the federal army, and he loved the Union deeply. Many times in the past he had deplored the agitation of both Northern and Southern "firebrands," and now he was asked to become associated with them. He reminded the Texans that he was yet a federal officer, that he was a Virginian and not a Texan, and that he reserved the right of making up his mind without pressure. Then he strode angrily from the room. The Texans did not hold him, probably because they felt that he would ultimately support the action of

Virginia, and they had nothing to gain by forcing on him a hasty decision.

Charles Anderson, one of Lee's intimate San Antonio friends, later wrote that Lee came to him directly from this interview, still wrathful. He quoted Lee as saying that the Texans had threatened to hold his personal effects so that he could not leave the city unless he declared his support of the Confederacy but that they had not placed him under arrest. If Anderson would take care of his baggage and send it on to him later, he would depart the next morning for Washington. He cautioned his friend, however, that he wanted to make clear his view on secession. If Virginia seceded, he would support its action with his sword, and, if necessary, with his life, although he did not believe in secession as a constitutional right. Anderson stated that he did not challenge Lee's position, although he was an ardent pro-Unionist, and that he readily agreed to care for his baggage. It is difficult, however, to accept at face value Anderson's remembrance of Lee's declaration, for certainly Lee's actions were more conservative after he reached Washington, when he hoped that he would never have to draw his sword against the Union.

On the day following this incident Lee quietly boarded the stage for Indianola, where he could take ship for New Orleans on his way back to Washington. General Scott had ordered him to report to him personally, and to Washington he would go.

Units of the Second Cavalry had also left their border posts preparatory to departing from Texas. For years the troopers had stood between the settlers and the Indians, "protecting each at times from the wrong-doings of the other." Lee's inspiring zeal and devotion to duty had developed a high morale in the officers and men of his regiment. By 1861 both civilians and soldiers of Texas regarded the Second Cavalry as the élite regiment of the border, and frontiersmen generally expressed alarm that state troops now proposed to supplant these seasoned soldiers. The state press, too, lamented the imminent clash between these two classes of border defenders, saying justly that "the regular army had made with its best blood many places within the state holy and almost classic ground, and black indeed would be that page in Texas history which should record such contests."

Twiggs's surrender agreement had put the Second Cavalry on an uncertain footing. Captains Oakes, Stoneman, and Whiting met at Fort Inge to consider uniting their three companies to march through Indian Territory to Jefferson Barracks, but they found that all serviceable transportation had been removed from the Texas posts and that subsistence stores were barely sufficient for a march to the Gulf coast.

To make matters worse, the Second Cavalry was without a commanding officer during this crisis. Colonel Johnston was at San Francisco, commanding the Department of California, and Majors Thomas and Van Dorn were on leaves of absence.

In February, 1861, Companies B, D, H, and I started for the coast and were soon followed by the others. When one detachment arrived at San Antonio, it marched through the principal streets with the regimental standard and company guidons displayed and its band playing "Yankee Doodle" and "Hail, Columbia." Some of its enlisted men cut down the Texas flag from above the

East front of Arlington, showing Federal troops in occupation

Alamo and used it to make head-streamers for the train mules. Still the troopers were permitted to leave without a brush with the state troops. However, on the day following the sailing of this group from Indianola, a Confederate force entered the town and captured the remaining transport, together with all the troops who had not yet sailed, who now were paroled as prisoners of war.

What happened at Camp Cooper and Fort Mason, the two posts where Lee had been stationed, was typical of other posts. Captain Innis N. Palmer with Companies D and H, Second Cavalry, left Camp Cooper on February 21, 1861, bound for the Texas coast, in keeping with Twiggs's surrender agreement; and four days later Captain Stephen D. Carpenter surrendered the post to Colonel W. C. Dalrymple of the state troops and marched away with Company I, First United States Infantry. Captain Richard W. Johnson hauled down the flag from above Fort Mason on March 21 and with two companies of the Second Cavalry, started his long journey to the Texas coast. Taking one final glance backward, he saw dense, heavy smoke rising from burning post buildings, probably fired by his own men.

Lee's departure for Washington brought to an end his military services in Texas, services that not only had established a proud tradition, the Second Cavalry's marked *esprit de corps,* but had matured his own spirit as well. Lee was as ignorant of the great contribution he had made as of the effect that Texas had had on him. Both officers and enlisted men under him took great pride in their "Colonel Lee," as personifying the finest qualities of American soldiery. Moreover, so long as there was a Texas border, lonely military posts, and men to defend them, the high principles, selfless devotion to duty, and sense of justice which Lee exemplified were criteria for leadership.

In return, the long months spent in lonely outposts, with time for meditation and introspection, had ripened Lee, although he no doubt often felt that his Texas years were bringing him to a dead end. No great military advance had been accomplished, and since 1856 he had known little more than frustration of his aims and purposes. He had sought to punish the Comanche marauders but had not found them; he had attempted to keep Katumse and his people "on the white man's road," but they had deserted it; he had started to build Camp Cooper into a modern post but was transferred to another field of service before his work was completed; he had spent fruitless months attending court-martials; and he had sought unsuccessfully to capture the slippery Cortinas. As a climax, while he was "lost on the frontier," the brigadier generalship proposed by his friends was denied him, although official Washington had readily admitted that he richly deserved reward and that he was "America's very best soldier." Less modest men had pushed their own interests and had been favored while Lee spent months of vain waiting for promotion. Moreover, during the time when he was many miles from home, he had been harrassed by mounting and pressing domestic problems, not the least among them the serious illness of his wife and the death of his father-in-law.

In "Walden," Thoreau, quoting Damodara, said: "There are none happy in the world but beings who enjoy freely a vast horizon." In western Texas Lee was awed by the "magnificient distances" and leaned to appreciate the sweep of the country. Yet silence and loneliness oppressed him at times, and once he wrote that nothing was drawn from his "desert of dullness." Nevertheless, almost imperceptibly, much had been drawn—amazing patience, forbearance, human understanding, and deep spiritual insight. His intense feeling for his family, his home, and Virginia had ripened into near passion.

When Lee arrived at Arlington on March 1, 1861, he entered a new period of his life, which carries us beyond the bounds of this narrative, and which his biographer, Douglas Southall Freeman, describes in graphic detail. Lee was permitted to know only a few weeks of affection and comfort of family and home before he was swept into the vortex of war. On March 1 General Twiggs was dismissed from the army because of his Texas surrender; Colonel E. V. Sumner of the First Cavalry was promoted to brigadier general to succeed him; and Lee was given Sumner's former command and rank. On April 7 Lee's old comrade of Mexican War days, P. G. T. Beauregard, this time with the Confederate Army, ordered his men to fire on Fort Sumter, which, two weeks later, surrendered. Now that war had come, President Abraham Lincoln, with Secretary Cameron's approval, authorized Francis Preston Blair, Sr., to offer Lee command of a federal army of up to 100,000 men to invade the South. Declining the offer, Lee hastened to General Scott to tell him of his refusal.

"Lee, you have made the greatest mistake of your life," Scott is reported to have told him, although for some time he had privately thought that Lee might refuse to bear arms against the South. He added that if Lee proposed to resign from the United States Army, he ought to do so at once, for his present position as a federal officer was "equivocal."

Two days later Lee sent Scott his written resignation, expressing at the same time his deep appreciation of the many favors the General had shown him and saying that he would have presented his resignation at once but for the struggle it had cost him. He added the hope that he would never again have to draw his sword. Months later Mrs. Lee wrote a friend, "My husband has wept tears of blood over this terrible war, but as a man of honor and a Virginian, he must follow the destiny of his state."

On the same day that Lee resigned his commission, he wrote his brother, Smith, and his sister, Mrs. Marshall, explaining his action. To Mrs. Marshall he expressed his love for the Union and his loyalty as an American citizen, but, he said, "I have not been able to make up my mind to raise my hand against my relatives, my children, my home." Had he accepted Blair's tentative offer, he would have had to do just that. He added that he hoped the time would never come when he should be called upon to draw his sword again except in defense of his native state.

But the time did come speedily. Already Lincoln had sent out, on April 15, a ringing call for 75,000 volunteers, to be used presumably in coercing the South. Then the long-threatened storm of war struck, and Lee was forced to take a more militant stand. He realized that Virginia could not escape invasion, for it was just across the Potomac from Washington. The state had seceded from the Union on April 18 and now called on Lee to help repel the massing enemy. The occasion which he had hoped would never arrive was upon him with terrible swiftness, and, the die cast, he accepted the call unhesitatingly. On April 22, at Governor John Letcher's request, he boarded a train for Richmond to accept a commission in the service of Virginia, which ultimately brought him to the command of the Southern armies.

Lee had deliberately made his decision to support Virginia in its hour of need. He had sheathed his sword to retire to private life; but the Union had gone to pieces in a stormy sea on the rock of sectional discord. Lincoln was trying to reunite it by force of arms, military despotism, Lee thought, and Virginia now called upon him to defend not only its sovereign rights but also his home and his family. Lee felt that he had no greater obligation, save to his God, than to defend them. Therefore, he sped toward Richmond to answer the summons, turning his back on the flag he yet loved.

Lee's Texas service had brought his physical, mental, and spiritual powers into complete co-ordination. Now he was master of himself and had reached the zenith of his military fitness—mentally alert, with broad experience and sound knowledge of the science of war. Soon the Confederacy would see him as his Fort Mason admirer had described him: "so calm, so serene, so thoughtful, and so commanding."

Bibliography

1. Manuscripts

THE MOST IMPORTANT MANUSCRIPT COLLECTION throwing light on Lieutenant Colonel Robert E. Lee's Texas experiences from 1856 to 1861 is that of his family papers of two hundred or more pieces, now under restriction in the Division of Manuscripts, Library of Congress, Washington, D. C. For the most part these papers consist of letters written by Lee and other members of his family. But in addition there are miscellaneous papers, including three helpful memoranda books. Book No. 1 contains a few roughly drawn maps, a field note in July, 1856, from Major Earl Van Dorn to Lee, and Lee's incomplete letter copies from December 3, 1838, to February 4, 1860. Letters of the period from May 3, 1842, to April 11, 1860, are also in his "Letter Book, No. 2." Lee's "Memo. Book, No. 3" is a valuable supplement to his family letters. Within its first thirty-four pages are Mexican War sketches and drawings, of Monclova, Vera Cruz, and other places. Then, next, is a brief day-by-day journal, with wide gaps, running from July, 1855, to February, 1861. Following the daily entries are brief commentaries on "Sectarianism," "Education," "Geology," and "Engineering." Elsewhere in the Division of Manuscripts are a few other Lee letters: e.g., Lee to Van Dorn, July 3, 1860 (Acc. 1015); Lee to Mrs. W. Louis Marshall, April 20, 1861 (Acc. 4628); and Lee to General Winfield Scott, April 20, 1861 (Acc. 4627).

The George Denison Papers, a small collection covering the years 1854 to 1862 are also in the Division of Manuscripts.

Denison was a New England school teacher who lived in San Antonio during the period of Lee's stay in Texas. His portrayals of the Alamo City's life and conditions are excellent.

Lee's official letters, reports, and orders, written while he was stationed in Texas as lieutenant colonel of the Second Cavalry, together with other military papers bearing on the Texas border problem, are filed in the War Records Division, National Archives, Washington, D. C. They are found in such categories as "Letters Received," and "Consolidated File," and include such items as inspection and reconnaissance reports, regimental returns, and other papers bundled with the Secretary of War's annual report. More than one thousand pieces bear on the Texas border problem during Lee's stay from 1856 to 1861.

Other divisions of the National Archives house additional materials. The Division of Interior Department Archives, the Office of Indian Affairs, parallels the War Records Division in point of annual reports of the Commissioner of Indian Affairs, divisional superintendents, and agents—all bearing directly on tribal affairs, raiding, reservation problems, settler grievances, and border relations. And, finally, the Division of Photographic Archives and the Division of Maps and Charts yield photographs and maps of the sort used in this study.

Supplementing these National Archives records, other papers are found in two depositories at Austin, Texas. In the Texas State Library, in the Capitol are the Lea letters; the unpublished "Memoirs of John Salmon Ford" (vol. 5), relating to the Cortinas war and giving Ford's estimate of Lee; and the "Executive Record Book, Governor Samuel Houston, 1859–1861," covering the same period; and the letters and reports received by the Texas governors, 1856–1861, showing the desperate plight of the border settlements and the movements of the state troops.

Interesting details of the operations of the Clear Fork

Comanche reservation, the Sanaco-Katumse rivalry, and bits of Neighbor's correspondence are in Robert S. Neighbors Papers, 1857–59 (twenty-nine documents), Archives, University of Texas Library.

Still other miscellaneous papers of Lee were furnished the author by Mr. Henry Sayles, Jr., Abilene, Texas; Acting Librarian Richard H. Shoemaker, Cyrus Hall McCormick Library, Washington and Lee University, Lexington, Virginia; Mr. C. L. Greenwood, Austin, Texas; and Colonel M. L. Crimmins, San Antonio, Texas.

2. *Federal Documents*

FEDERAL DOCUMENTS examined by the author bearing on Lee's army services are mainly the House and Senate *Executive Documents. House Executive Document No. 6,* 30 Congress, 1 session, Vols. I and II, contain official papers, diplomatic and military, of the Mexican War period. "The Purchase of Camels" is the subject of *Senate Executive Document No. 62,* 34 Congress, 3 session; and scouting reports, troop changes, settler complaints, Indian raids, and the Cortinas war are the miscellaneous listings in *House Executive Document No. 2,* 32 Congress, 1 session, Part I; *Executive Document* (No house or number given), 34 Congress, 1 session, Vol. I, Part II; *Senate Executive Document No. 5,* 34 Congress, 3 session, Vol. II; *Senate Executive Document No. 1,* 35 Congress, 2 session, Vol. II; *Senate Executive Document No. 11,* 35 Congress, 1 session, Vol. II; *House Executive Document No. 52,* 36 Congress, 1 session; *Senate Executive Document No. 1,* 36 Congress, 2 session, Vol. II; and *House Executive Document No. 81,* 36 Congress, 1 session.

3. *Newspapers*

FAIRLY COMPLETE NEWSPAPER FILES of the Library of Congress, the Texas State Library, and the University of Texas Library are useful for the period 1856 to 1861. Among those headlining Indian atrocities, state and federal troop move-

ments, and border turmoil are the Belton (Texas) *Indepen-
dent,* 1857–59; the St. Louis (Missouri) *Republican,* 1859–60;
the *Texas State Gazette* (Austin), 1856–81; the San Antonio
(Texas) *Ledger and Texan,* 1860; the Dallas (Texas) *Herald,*
1856–61; the Clarksville (Texas) *Standard,* 1856–57, and
1860–61; and the *Southern Intelligencer* (Austin, Texas),
1856-61.

4. Lee Biographies and Memoirs

AMONG ALL THE BIOGRAPHIES that have been written about
General Robert E. Lee only one is of definitive, scholarly
value–Douglas Southall Freeman, *R. E. Lee* (4 vols., New
York, 1935). Volume I, pages 1 to 461 of this fine work in-
cludes a discussion and an excellent documentation of Lee's
family, his early rearing and training at West Point, his assignments with the Corps of Engineers, and his Mexican
War and Texas experiences. A reproduction of a part of
Lee's family correspondence, supplementing Freeman's narrative, may be found in three other studies: Emily V. Mason,
Popular Life of General Robert E. Lee (Baltimore, 1872);
Fitzhugh Lee, *General Lee* (New York, 1886); and J. William Jones, *Life and Letters of Robert Edward Lee, Soldier
and Man* (Washington, 1906). Of this group only Fitzhugh
Lee's account is of material value beyond the reproduction
of Lee's letters.

Other Lee biographies that should be given passing
mention are: Philip Alexander Bruce, *Robert E. Lee (American Crisis Biographies,* Philadelphia, 1907); Major General
J. F. C. Fuller, *Grant and Lee: A Study in Personality and
Generalship* (New York, 1933); Bradley Gilman, *Robert E.
Lee* (New York, 1919); Burton J. Hendrick, *The Lees of
Virginia* (Boston, 1935); Captain Robert E. Lee, Jr., *Recol-
lections and Letters of General Robert E. Lee* (New York,
1905); A. L. Long, *Memoirs of Robert E. Lee; His Military
and Personal History* (Philadelphia and Washington, 1887);
James D. McCabe, Jr., *Life and Campaigns of General Robert*

E. Lee (Atlanta, Philadelphia, Cincinnati, St. Louis, 1870); William P. Trent, *Robert E. Lee* (Boston, 1899); Henry Alexander White, *Robert E. Lee and the Southern Confederacy, 1807–1870* (New York and London, 1897) and Robert W. Winston, *Robert E. Lee, A Biography* (New York, 1934). Beyond an incidental fact here and there to weigh and evaluate and the reproduction of Lee letters and a part of his "Memo. Book, No. 3," these references are of little value to the research student interested only in Lee's pre–Civil War years.

5. *Miscellaneous*

WITHIN THIS CATEGORY OF MATERIALS are sundry books and magazines picturing life on the pre–Civil War Texas border, the wild Comanches, frontier forts, overland trails, roads and freighting, and the observations of Lee's contemporaries. Three army registers of great value are: F. B. Heitman, *Historical Register and Dictionary of the United States Army* (2 vols., Washington, 1903); T. H. S. Hammersley, *Complete Regular Army Register of the United States* (Washington, 1880); and Brevet Major General George W. Cullum, *Biographical Register of Officers and Graduates of United States Military Academy, at West Point, N. Y.* (2 vols., New York, 1868–79). The general narrative of William Addleman Ganoe, *The History of the United States Army* (New York, 1924) should be read with these for a general sweep of military problems and policies. George F. Price, comp., *Across the Continent with the Fifth Cavalry* (New York, 1883) is of primary importance, since the Fifth Cavalry was organized as the Second Cavalry. This book is invaluable for its narrative of the border services rendered by the Second Cavalry and for its brief sketches of the regiment's officers.

There are also available a few biographies and reminiscences of Lee's fellow officers and friends, including comments on Lee. Lee at Camp Cooper is briefly considered in J. B. Hood, *Advance and Retreat* (New Orleans, 1880); and

William Preston Johnston, *The Life of General Albert Sidney Johnston* (New York, 1878). Lee's brief stay at Fort Mason and at San Antonio is referred to in Brigadier General R. W. Johnson, *A Soldier's Reminiscences in Peace and War* (Philadelphia, 1886);———, *Memoirs of General George H. Thomas* (Philadelphia, 1881); and Charles Anderson, *Texas Before and on the Eve of the Rebellion* (Cincinnati, 1884).

Contemporary Mexican War views, and a part of the diplomatic and military correspondence of the period, are seen in four narratives, all relating to the expeditions of Taylor, Wool, and Scott. Those of some importance are Francis Baylies, *Narrative of Major-General Wool's Campaign in Mexico* (Albany, 1851); J. Frost, *The Mexican War and its Warriors* (New Haven, 1850); and Edward K. Mansfield, *The Mexican War; A History of Its Origin* (New York, 1848). Of lesser value is William Jay, *A Review of the Causes and Consequences of the Mexican War* (Boston, 1849).

The author used articles in three regional magazines. Decca Lamar West, "Robert E. Lee in Texas," in *Texas Monthly,* April, 1930, 323–39, is an excellent sketch. But of greater value are several articles in the *West Texas Historical Association Yearbook* discussing the Texas border army, transportation problems, Texas roads and trails, army posts, and Lee and his contemporaries. They are W. C. Holden, "Frontier Defense in Texas during the Civil War," in Vol. IV (June, 1928), 16–32; R. N. Richardson, "The Comanche Reservation in Texas," in Vol. V (June, 1929), 43–66; Lenora Barrett, "Transportation, Supplies, and Quarters for the West Texas Frontier Under the Federal Military System, 1848-1861," in *ibid.,* 87-100; Arrie Barrett, "Western Frontier Forts of Texas," in Vol. VII (June, 1931), 115–40; Colonel M. L. Crimmins, "What General Robert E. Lee's Generals Thought of Him," in Vol. XII (July, 1936), 95–100; ———, "Major Earl Van Dorn in Texas," in Vol. XVI (October, 1940), 121–30; C. C. Rister, "The Border Post of

Phantom Hill," in Vol. XIV (October, 1938), 3–14; Colonel M. L. Crimmins, Camp Cooper and Fort Griffin, Texas, in Vol. XVII (October, 1941), 32–44; ———, "General John E. Wool in Texas," in Vol. XVIII (October, 1942), 47–54; J. W. Williams, "Military Roads of the 1850's in Central West Texas," in *ibid.*, 77–92; Colonel M. L. Crimmins, "The First Line of Army Posts Established in West Texas in 1849," in Vol. XIX (October, 1943), 121–28; and R. C. Crane, "Major George H. Thomas on the Trail of Indians in 1860," in Vol. XX (October, 1944), 77–86. Colonel Crimmins also has, in addition, "Colonel Robert E. Lee's Report on Indian Combats in Texas," in *Southwestern Historical Quarterly*, Vol. XXXIX, No. 3 (July, 1935), 21–33.

One may find a number of miscellaneous items of interest in such books as: Charles Merritt Barnes, *Combats and Conquests of Immortal Heroes* (San Antonio, 1910); J. De Cordova, *Texas; Her Resources and Her Public Men* (Philadelphia, 1858); R. B. Marcy, *Thirty Years of Army Life on the Border* (New York, 1866); James P. Newcomb, *Sketches of Secession Times in Texas and Journal of Travel from Texas through Mexico to California, and a History of the "Box Colony"* (San Francisco, 1863), 10–11; W. B. Parker, *Notes Taken During the Expedition Commanded by Capt. R. B. Marcy, U. S. A. Through Unexplored Texas in the Summer and Fall of 1854* (Philadelphia, 1856); George F. Price, *Across the Continent with the Second Cavalry* (New York, 1883); R. N. Richardson, *The Comanche Barrier to South Plains Settlement* (Glendale, California, 1928); Carl Coke Rister, *The Southwestern Frontier, 1865–1881* (Cleveland, 1928); ———, *Border Captives* (Norman, Oklahoma, 1940); and Walter Prescott Webb, *The Texas Rangers; A Century of Frontier Defense* (Boston and New York, 1935).

Index

Alamo: massacre at the, 7

Anadarkos: on Brazos reservation, 27

Anderson, Charles: Lee's property custodian, 161

Arapahoes: war on the border, 42

Arlington, Virginia: Lee becomes master of, 5; neglect of, 96; Lee improves, 97–98

Army wife: trial of, 67

Bainbridge, Colonel: Lee meets on Rio Grande, 66

Barnard, Brevet Major Jonathan: succeeds Lee at West Point, 14

Baylor, John R.: Comanche agent, 16; services of on reservation, 34–35; dismissal of, 138; leads settlers against Comanche reservation, 138–39

Beauregard, P.G.T.: 165

Big Springs, Texas: Lee visits, 50

Blizzard, Texas: 15

Boerne, Texas: 62

Boggs, William R.: 13

Border posts: distances apart, 91; see also forts and camps

Brackett, Captain A. G.: aids Lee against Cortinas, 116; visits Reynosa, 121

Bradford, Captain James A. G.: 62; at Ringgold Barracks court-martial, 66

Bradfute, Captain William R: with Lee's reconnaissance, 43

Brazos Agency: Indian bands at, 27; Mansfield comments on, 55

Bronte, Texas: 43

Brown County, Texas: Indian raid in, 143–44

Brown, John: raid of, 98–99

Brownsville, Texas: Cortinas' home near, 107; Cortinas raids, 107–16

Brownsville Tigers: 111

Buffalo Hump (Comanche chief): 34

Butterfield Trail: 144

Cabrera, Tomás: Cortinas's second in command, 110

Caddos: on Brazos reservation, 27

Caldwell, Captain J. N.: 56

Camels: Wayne imports, 80; Big Bend experiment with, 131 ff.

Camel's Hump Mountain: 135–36

Cameron, Simon: 165

Camp Cooper, Texas: Texas legislature creates, 4; Second Cavalry unit occupies, 16; life at, 38–39; expedition from, 40; Lee returns to (July, 1856), 52; sickness at, 54; Lt. Dick dies at, 55; Col. Joseph K. F. Mansfield inspects, 55–58; Minter's drawing of, 57; drought broken at, 60; Lee assumes command of, 82–83; drought again, 83; Major and Mrs. Thomas visit, 85–86; Comanches threaten, 89; failing water supply, 89–90; Bigg's report on, 90–91; Indian hostility at (Aug., 1858), 137 ff.; abandoned as reservation, 140; stage road by, 145; expeditions from, 144–47; Cynthia Ann Parker brought to, 147–48; surrenders to Dalrymple, 163

Camp Holmes, Indian Territory: treaty (1835), 59

Camp Hudson, Texas: camels at, 132

Camp Johnson, Texas: Indian village near, 25

Camp Verde, Texas: Second Cavalry company at, 53, 116

Capistran, Don Macedonio: 110

Capron, Horace: 25

Carlisle Barracks, Pennsylvania: 15

Carpenter, Captain Stephen D.: 163

Castroville, Texas: sketch of, 62–63

Cerro Gordo, Mexico: battle at, 10

Chambliss, Lieutenant William P.: with Second Cavalry, 14

Chapman, Colonel: on Ringgold Barracks court-martial, 66

Cheyennes: war on border, 142

Childe, Mrs. Edward Vernon: death of, 54–55

Churubusco, Mexico: battle at, 10

Clarkson, Mrs. Kate Merrett: favored by Lee, 101

Clear Fork of Brazos River: Comanche Agency on, 4; Camp Cooper on, 4; Penateka council at, 29 ff.; Lee rides along, 86–87; Lee spends July Fourth on, 47

Colorado: Indian raids in, 142; settlements advance in, 143

Comanches: Katumse's Penatekas, 19 ff.; Sanaco's band, 28 ff.; reservation for, 32 ff.; Buffalo Hump's band escapes, 34; Yamparikas raid, 36; Tanimas' raids, 40; woman captured, 48–49; raids, 137, 139, 143, 145–46

Comanche reservation: Mansfield comments on, 55–56

Comancheros: trade with Indians, 146–47

Comanche trail: 136

Cortinas, Juan Nepomuceno: early life of, 106–107; San José Rancho of, 107; raids Brownsville, 108; defeats Brownsville posse, 112; high tide of success of, 112; federal troops rout, 112–13; later activities, 128

Contreras, Mexico: battle at, 10

Creole: Lee's horse, 8–9; Lee rides on Mexican battle fields, 11

Crimmins, Colonel M. L.: 9

Crittenden, J. J.: 154

Custis, George Washington Parke (Lee's father-in-law): 5; death of, 95; Lee probates will of, 97

Custis, Mary: *see* Mary Custis Lee

Dalrymple, Colonel W. C.: occupies Camp Cooper, 163

Darrow, Mrs. Caroline: 159

Davis, Secretary Jefferson: recommends new cavalry regiment, 13

Delaware Scouts: aid Lee, 42 ff.

Devine, Thomas: 160

D'Hannis, Texas: 63

Dick, Lieutenant George M.: death of, 54

Doss (Delaware Scout): 145

Double Mountains: Lee camps near, 45; Indian camp destroyed near, 48

Drinkard, Colonel: 98

Eagle, Lieutenant Robert N.: court-martial of, 82

Eagle Pass, Texas: description of, 64; Cortinas reported near, 114

Echols, Lieutenant William H.: camel experiments of, 131

Edinburg, Texas: Cortinas influences, 115

Evans, N. G.: assigned to Second

Cavalry, 14; Camp Cooper commandant, 148

Field, Charles W.: with Second Cavalry, 14
Five Civilized Tribes: westward advance, 143
Floyd, Secretary of War John B.: 88; orders Lee to Harper's Ferry, 98
Ford, Major John S.: at Bolsa Bend, 113; describes Lee, 121; invades Reynosa, Mexico, 122; Lee chides, 122; leads expedition against Indians, 140; confederate officer, 159
Fort Brown, Texas: Porter's trial transferred to, 70; Cortinas takes over, 108–109; Lee visits, 123–27
Fort Chadbourne, Texas: Lee's troops at, 40
Fort Clark, Texas: units of Second Cavalry for, 53
Fort Davis, Texas: camel expedition to, 136
Fort Duncan, Texas: description of, 64–65
Fort Hamilton, New York: Lee at, 5, 6
Fort Inge, Texas: Lee visits, 63
Fort Laramie, Wyoming: massacre near, 13
Fort Leavenworth, Kansas: 15
Fort Mason, Texas: distance from Camp Cooper, 4; Colonel Johnston's headquarters at (Jan. 1, 1856), 16; in new scheme of defense, 53; court-martial at, 92; Lee commands, 150; life at, 151; drawing of, 152; abandoned, 163
Fort Riley, Kansas: 15
Fraser, Captain William D.: Wool's Engineer, 7–8
Fredericksburg, Texas: Lee stops at, 62
Freeman, Douglas Southall: 5

García, General Guadalupe: 108; complains to Lee, 123
Gaenslen, Dr. John G.: at Camp Cooper, 54; attends Camp Cooper sick, 85
Garrard, K.: with Second Cavalry, 14
Glasscock County, Texas: Major Thomas's expedition in, 145
Glavaecke, Adolphus: seeks Cortinas's arrest, 107 ff.
Gracie, Archibald: 13
Gratiot, Charles: Lee under, 5
Grattan Massacre (1854): 13

Hardee, Major W. J.: leaves Camp Cooper, 19–21
Harper's Ferry, Virginia: John Brown's raid at, 98–99
Heintzelman, Major S. P.: reports on Cortinas, 108; at Bolsa Bend, 113
Holman, Lieutenant J. H.: 133
Houston, Governor Sam: writes of border conditions, 102; filibuster plan, 102–106; sketch of, 103; writes Secretary Floyd about Indian disturbances, 103; reports on border, 126; sends commissioners to Camp Cooper, 140
Hood, John B.: Lee serves with in Mexico, 13; with Second Cavalry, 14; compliments Lee, 87–88
Howard, O. O.: 13
Howard County, Texas: Major Thomas's expedition in, 145

Indian raids: 117, 125
Indian Territory: Indian village destroyed in, 141
Iron County, Texas: Major Thomas's expedition in, 145

Jalapa, Mexico: battle at, 10
Jefferson Barracks, Missouri: Second Cavalry at, 14–15

Jenifer, Lieutenant Walter H.: 50

Johnson, Captain Richard W.: with Second Cavalry, 14; with Thomas expedition (1860), 144; abandons Fort Mason, 163

Johnston, Albert Sidney: Colonel of Second Cavalry, 14; court-martial duty, 15; goes to Texas with Second Cavalry, 16; Lee dines with, 17; opinion on Comanche expedition, 42; Lee dines in home of, 80; to Washington, 92; leads Utah expedition, 94

Johnston, General Joseph E.: comments on Lee, 87; promoted, 153

Jones, Captain John M.: 91

Jones, Captain Samuel: at court-martial of Major Porter, 66

Kansas: Indian raids in, 142; advance of frontier, 143

Katumse: visits Lee, 19–20; on Concho River, 25; rivalry with Sanaco, 28; on reservation, 34–36; opposes tribesmen, 137–38; attempts to appease angry settlers, 139

King, Captain John H.: 56

Kiowas: raid Texas settlements, 142

Kotsotekas: village of, destroyed, 140–41

La Bolsa Bend, Texas: battle of, 112

La Ebronal, Texas: battle of, 112–13

Laredo, Texas: Lee visits, 118

Larharn, Francis W.: customs collector, 109–10

Lea, A. M.: filibustering proposal, 102 ff.

Lea, P. L.: filibustering plan of, 101 ff.

Lee, Agnes: 5; inherits money, 97

Lee, Annie: 5; inherits wealth, 97

Lee, Custis: inherits property, 97; Washington assignment of, 100

Lee, Henry ("Light Horse Harry"): 4

Lee, Fitzhugh: commissioned, 95; inherits property, 97; father's advice, 130

Lee, Lieutenant Fitzhugh (Colonel Lee's nephew): duels with Comanche, 143–44; with Thomas expedition (1860), 144

Lee, George Washington Custis: 5

Lee, Mary: 5; inherits wealth, 97

Lee, Mary Carter (Lee's mother): 4

Lee, Mary Custis (Mrs. Robert E. Lee): marries, 5; Lee writes about battle scenes, 10; Lee writes about training at Jefferson Barracks, 15; interested in Lee's promotion, 60; Lee writes about Christmas, 74–75; Lee gives advice, 75; illness of, 96–97

Lee, Mildred: 5; father writes about cats, 79; inherits money, 97; Lee advises to read nonfiction, 59

Lee, Robert Edward, Jr.: 5; Lee advises courses to study, 59; inherits property, 97

Lee, Robert E.: Texas stations of, *vii;* influence of Texas on, *viii,* 17; arrives at Camp Cooper (April 9, 1856), 3–4; early training of, 4; first assignments, 4–5; marries, 5; joins Wool at San Antonio, 7; serves Wool in Mexico, 8–9; with Scott's army, 9–12; Mexican War honors of, 10; at homa again, 12; superintendent of West Point, 13; with Second Cavalry, 14; with Second Cavalry at Louisville and Jefferson Barracks, 14–15; on court-martial duty, 15; Katumse visits, 19–20; inspects Second Cavalry, 21–23;

reconnaissance, 42 ff.; entertains the McArthurs at Camp Cooper, 58; chides Mrs. Lee for her efforts at his promotion, 60; appointed on Ringgold Barracks court-martial session, 61 ff.; travels down Rio Grande, 64 ff.; to Fort Brown, 70; on slavery agitation, 72–73; visits Matamoros, 74; calls on Mrs. King, 75–76; visits mustanger camp, 77–78; writes Mildred about cats, 78; back in San Antonio, 79–80; dines with Johnstons and Thomases, 80; sees camel experiment, 80; returns to Camp Cooper (April 18, 1857), 81; entertains Mrs. Thomas, 84; reads burial service, 85–86; relations with fellow officers, 87–88; transferred to San Antonio (July 16, 1857), 92; at Fredericksburg, 92; succeeds Twiggs, 94; returns to Virginia, 95; probates father-in-law's will, 97; calls on President James Buchanan, 97; at Harper's Ferry, 98–99; arrives at San Antonio (Feb. 19, 1860), 100; at a San Antonio social, 101; instructed to hunt Cortinas, 116; travels to Rio Grande, 117 ff.; warns Governor Andres Treviño, 120; talks with Zepeda, 122; at Brownsville (April 12, 1860), 123; writes García, 123–24; as department commander, 131; relieved of department command, 149; at Fort Mason, 150–57; entertains the Lowes, 151–52; watches sectional strife, 154–55; reads Everett's *Life of Washington*, 154–55; on secession, 157–58; back in San Antonio, 158; surrenders commission and goes with the South, 165 ff.

Lee, William Fitzhugh: 5

Longoría, Agopita: 109–10
Luckett, Phillip N.: 160

McCulloch, Colonel Ben: 159
McCulloch, Henry E.: 159
McPherson, John B.: 13
Mansfield, Colonel Jas. K. F.: inspects Camp Cooper, 55–58
Manypenny, George W.: 59
Marcy, Captain Randolph B.: helps survey Comanche reservation, 4; survey of, 25 ff.; holds council with Comanches, 29 ff.; at Ringgold Barracks, 66
"Markie": Lee writes, 153
Matamoros, Mexico: Lee visits, 74; Cortinas reported at, 127
Maverick, Samuel A.: 160
Mexican War: outbreak of, 5–6; Taylor's movements, 6–7; Wool's campaign, 6–8; Scott's advance, 9–11
Mitchell County: Major Thomas's expedition in, 145
Mountain Pass, Texas: 43
Murphy, William: wounded, 146
Mustangs: capture of, 77–78
Mustangers: Rio Grande, 77

Neighbors, Robert S.: helps survey Comanche reservation, 4; survey of, 25; Lee confers with, 40–41
New Mexico: Indian raids in, 142; advance of frontier in, 143
New Orleans, Louisiana: Lee at, 100

O'Hara, Theodore: sketch of, 23; with Lee's reconnaissance, 40; joins Van Dorn near Double Mountains, 48–49; scout along the Concho, 50; transferred to Mason-Belknap road camp, 53

Palmer, Captain Innis N.: with Second Cavalry, 14; at Camp

Verde, 53, 163
Palo Alto, Texas: battle at (May 8, 1846), 7
Parker, Cynthia Ann: recapture of, 147 ff.; death of, 148
Pender, W. D.: 13
Peta Nacona: duels with Ross, 146
Phantom Hill, Texas: Lee visits, 42–43
Phifer, Charles W.: with Second Cavalry, 14
Pierce, President Franklin K.: asked to advance Lee in rank, 60
Polk, President James K.: 6
Porter, Major Giles: court-martial trial of, 61 ff.; court adjourns, 76
Prairie Flower (Topasannah—Cynthia Ann Parker's daughter): death of, 148
Price, Captain George F.: 144

Radziminski, Lieutenant Charles: accompanies Lee to Camp Cooper, 37–38
Ranchero: attacked, 113
Reagan County, Texas: Major Thomas's expedition in, 145
Resaca de la Palma, Texas: battle at, 7
Reynosa, Mexico: disturbance at, 120–22
Rio Grande City, Texas: Cortinas reported near, 119
Rio Grande River: Lee travels down, 65 ff.
Ringgold Barracks, Texas: court-martial at, 61 ff.; Cortinas reported near, 119; Lee visits, 120
Roby, Texas: 45; Lee spends Fourth of July near, 47
Ross, S. P.: 55; Indian campaign, 140; Comanche expedition, 147–48; duels with Peta Nacona, 147
Saltillo, Mexico: Wool's army near, 8–9
Sanaco (Penateka Comanche chief):

25; rivalry with Katumse, 28; dines with Marcy, 30–31; renews "talk" with March, 32–33; flight of, 33
San Antonio, Mexico: battle at, 10
San Antonio, Texas: in 1846, 7; Lee transferred to (July 16, 1857), 92; Olmsted describes, 92–94; Lee returns to, 100; life at, 129; Spanish life at, 129, 130–31; drought at, 150; in secession, 158 ff.
San Carlos Trail: 136
San Francisco Creek: camel expedition to, 137
Santa Anna: reported movements of, 9
Santa Fé Trail: Indian raids on, 59
Santa Rita Rancho: 110
Scott, General Winfield: Mexican campaign of, 9–12; compliments Lee, 88
Seawell, Colonel: on Ringgold Barracks court-martial, 66
Second Cavalry: creation of, 13; officers of, 14; marches to Texas, 16; personnel and equipment of, 23; Lee commands, 94; Thomas succeeds Lee, 95; spearhead of Indian campaign, 141; estimate of Texas services, 161–62
Shaw, Jim: Delaware scout, 43
Sheridan, Phil: 13
Sibley, Captain: 66
Smith, E. Kirby: with Second Cavalry, 14; with Lee's reconnaissance, 43 ff.
Sterling County, Texas: Major Thomas campaigns in, 145
Stoneman, George: with Second Cavalry, 14; at Camp Cooper, 22
Stuart, J. E. B. ("Jeb"): 13; at Harper's Ferry, 98–99
Sweetwater, Texas: 45

Tanimas: raids of, 40

Index

Tawakonies: on Brazos reservation, 27

Texas: in election of 1844, 6; defense line, 24; Indian reservations, 26–27; drought, 37–38; Lee impressed by, 69; climate of, 130; secession convention, 156; Second Cavalry leaves, 161 ff.

Texas Rangers: in Brownsville, 111; pursue Cortinas, 112 ff.; Houston praises, 125; destroy Kotsoteka village, 140–41

Thomas, General George H.: Lee serves with in Mexico, 13; assigned to Second Cavalry, 14; assigned on court-martial, 61; Lee travels with to Ringgold Barracks, 61–66; Lee dines in home of, 80; commands Second Cavalry, 95; at Camp Cooper, 144 ff.; leads expedition against Comanches, 144 ff.; wounded, 146

Tijerina, Don Miguel: 108, 110

Tobin, Captain W. G.: 111 ff.

Tonkawas: on Brazos reservation, 27

Tom Green County, Texas: Major Thomas's expedition in, 145

Tosh-e-weh (Penateka chief): 139

Twiggs, General D. M.: Lee succeeds as Texas commander, 94; learns of Cortinas, 109; illness of, 130; Indian policy, 140; succeeds Lee as departmental commander (Dec. 13, 1860), 149; surrenders Department of Texas, 159

Van Camp, Lieutenant Cornelius: at Camp Cooper, 137–39

Van Dorn, Major Earl: assigned to Second Cavalry, 14; at Camp Cooper, 22; with Lee's reconnaissance, 40; destroys Indian Camp, 48–49; scouts headwaters of Concho, 50–51; transferred to Mason-Belknap road camp, 53

Vera Cruz, Mexico: battle at, 10

Waite, Colonel Carlos A.: on Ringgold Barracks court-martial, 66; succeeds Twiggs as department commander, 159

Webb, Walter Prescott: mention, 106

Whiting, Captain Charles J.: at Camp Cooper, 22; at Fort Inge, 64

Wool, Brigadier General John E.: at San Antonio, 7; expedition of, 7–9

Yamparikas: raid of, 59

Zepeda (Mexican official): 121 ff.

183

CRAIG HALHAMMER

919 - 455 - 8000